The Complete Films of
Steve McQueen

Steve

THE COMPLETE FILMS OF

McQueen

Casey St. Charnez

A CITADEL PRESS BOOK
Published by Carol Publishing Group

First Carol Publishing Group Edition 1992

A Citadel Press Book
Published by Carol Publishing Group
Citadel Press is a registered trademark of Carol Communications, Inc.

Editorial Offices: 600 Madison Avenue, New York, NY 10022
Sales & Distribution Offices: 120 Enterprise Avenue, Secaucus, NJ 07094
In Canada: Canadian Manda Group, P.O. Box 920, Station U, Toronto,
Ontario, M8Z 5P9, Canada

Queries regarding rights and permissions should be addressed to:
Carol Publishing Group, 600 Madison Avenue, New York, NY 10022

Manufactured in the United States of America
ISBN 0-8065-1010-2

Designed by A. Christopher Simon

Carol Publishing Group books are available at special discounts
for bulk purchases, for sales promotions, fund raising, or
educational purposes. Special editions can also be created to
specifications. For details contact: Special Sales Department,
Carol Publishing Group, 120 Enterprise Ave., Secaucus, NJ 07094

10 9 8 7 6 5 4 3 2

Library of Congress Cataloging-in-Publication Data

St. Charnez, Casey.
    The complete films of Steve McQueen.

    1. McQueen, Steve, 1930-1980. 2. Moving-picture
actors and actresses--United States--Biography.
I. Title.
PN2287.M547S7 1984   791.43'75   84-19931

TO MY PARENTS

Acknowledgments

During the ten years of research on this book, a number of individuals and organizations have proved to be most helpful. Among them are: James Coburn; William K. Everson; David Foster; William A. Fraker; Ellen Clark Hayers; Arthur Knight; Denise McCluggage; Allan J. Wilson; Robert and Millicent Wise; Mae Wood; Patrick J. Sheehan, David Parker, and Joseph Balian of the Library of Congress; Monty Arnold and Lincoln Center Library for the Performing Arts; Ann Schlosser, Roxyanne Williams and American Film Institute Library; Library of the Academy of Motion Picture Arts and Sciences; Museum of Modern Art Film Research Library; University of Wisconsin; Bennett's Bookstore; Book City Collectibles; Cinemabilia; Hollywood Book and Poster; Hollywood Book Service; Larry Edmunds Book Store; The Memory Shop; Marlow's Bookshop; Stephen Randall, *L.A.* Magazine; Nanette Leonard, Allied Artists; Hal Sherman, 20th Century-Fox; and Lisa S. Harris. Many thanks to all for various favors graciously and generously tendered.

Contents

The Complete Films of
Steve McQueen

Marine McQueen, 1947.

Little Steve McQueen spent the first
eight years of his life growing up in
this house in Slater, Missouri.

12

The Beginning

If someone had wanted to make a movie of *The Steve McQueen Story*, it could only have starred Steve McQueen. Living a life far larger than most lives came naturally to a feisty kid whose biography sounds like the plot of *Boys Town*. The problem boy, clearly headed for a life of crime, who ran away from home only to emerge a multimillionaire movie star, his image in lives both real and reel that of the nonconformist adventure hero. A good guy. McQueen himself would have probably recommended Paul Newman for the part.

The movie would begin in Beech Grove, Indiana, a suburb of Indianapolis, where Terence Stephen McQueen was born on March 24, 1930. An Aries, Scorpio rising, for those who care.

He never knew his father, a mystery figure whose name is conjectured to be William McQueen. Named by his father for Steve Hall, a one-armed bookmaker pal, the young Steve fantasized that his father had been a stunt pilot and former Navy flier with General Chennault's Flying Tigers in China. Steve would tell

friends even decades later that his dad had been shot down somewhere in the Orient some time in 1939. The truth was that William McQueen had deserted his family when Steve was six months old, and that there was doubt as to whether his parents had been married. The ghost of this featureless father, whether dead now or still living, haunted Steve for most of his adult life, but his ongoing, decades-long search for William McQueen proved utterly futile.

When the former Julia Crawford found herself abandoned at age 19 in the middle of Indiana with the infant Stevie, surrounded by a dust-blown America still staggering with shock from the onslaught of the Depression, she made the decision to retain the name McQueen and to turn to her relatives for help. She sent the baby ahead to be reared by his great uncle, C. W. Thompson, and his wife, in the farming town of Slater, Missouri, a sleepy burg generally credited as McQueen's birthplace.

Schooling interested him little. He was never an academician, probably couldn't spell it, but his teachers noted an earthy native intelligence that got him through. He was distinctly nonverbal, then as ever.

At nine, he was reunited with his mother, back home again in Indiana. Another shadowy period ensued, dominated by the melodramatic figure of what Steve saw as his cruel stepfather, J. Berri, whom Julia had married to regain her footing and her son. Later Steve would credit Berri with hickory-switching him into honesty and responsibility; but the way Steve saw it as he was growing up, nobody understood him and he just wanted to get away. To be alone, to be left alone.

At 13, he said later, he lost his virginity. With whom or under what circumstances was never revealed to anyone. At 14, he was trying hard to run away and not get caught every time. Skirmishes with the law became the dominant theme of these early teenage years, and as he ran around with gangs playing at vandalism and petty theft, the Berris felt it was time to put a rein on Steve. With his own and his mother's consent, he was admitted at age 15, under the name Steve Berri, into Boys Republic of Chino, California.

Rarely is a turning point in a young life so clearly defined as the moment Steve entered Chino, a 211-acre facility peppered with eucalyptus and palm that was the inspiration for Father Edward Flanagan's more famous Boys Town. The whole approach to Steve's residency lay in the fact that he had been admitted, rather than committed, to the facility, and even though he was serial number 3188, he was also a human being, directed firmly and finally onto the proverbial right path. He stayed at Chino 18 months, and despite the numerous escape attempts and fistfights, practically mandatory for a guy of his bent, he credited the experience with straightening him out. Years later, he would return to Chino as Steve McQueen the movie star, armed with endowments and advice.

After leaving Boys Republic, his life unfolded like the pages of a script. Feeling grown up now, though still only 16, he didn't want to return to the rule of his mother, now widowed and living in New York City, or to the lure of his old street ways, no matter how tempting.

Therefore, as soon as he was legally graduated from ninth grade, he hit the road.

The road: First he hitchhiked to New Orleans, signing on as a deck-ape on a tanker headed for South America. He jumped ship in the Dominican Republic, worked his way back to the United States, and got jobs as a grunt in the oil fields of Corpus Christi and Waco, Texas. He was a runner for a brothel, then a carnival huckster for a road show that traveled to Canada, where he got a job topping trees as a lumberjack.

In April, 1947, he'd had enough of the itinerant laborer's life and enlisted in the Marines. He served through April, 1950, at Camp Pendleton as a tank driver and mechanic, his first exposure to auto work, which he found with a shock and embraced with a passion heretofore reserved for women. He was proud of what he called "the only souped-up tank in the joint." But he also had trouble. He was busted from Pfc. to Private seven times, and spent some 41 days in the brig for extending a weekend pass into a two-week AWOL, and for getting into a scrape with the Shore Patrol when they called him on it. He left the Marines by his own volition soon thereafter, with an honorable discharge from Camp Lejeune, North Carolina.

His next stop was back in New York City again, the place he'd seen that entranced him the most. He moved into a $19 per month coldwater flat that summer of 1950, and spent his workday time picking up such odd jobs as leather-cutter for a sandalmaker, as well as becoming a vendor of ballpoint pens, encyclopedias, and artificial flowers at one time or another. He was mechanic for his own taxi and repaired televisions in the Village. Off-duty time was spent at poker and with women.: "For the first time in my life," he once looked back, "I was really exposed to music, culture, a little kindness, a little sensitivity. It was a way of life where people talked out their problems instead of punching you." It was said with revelation.

He also bought his first motorcycle.

And he began to act.

One element of McQueen's acting persona that made him such a credible star in the generation to come was his ability to choose roles directly reflecting his own life's path. Able to recognize his interests in life as foundations upon which a screen image could be built, he would see his teenage gang years reflected in *Somebody Up There Likes Me*, his stint in the Armed Forces portrayed in *The War Lover* and *Soldier in the Rain*, his compulsive anti-authoritarian attitude made charming in *The Great Escape*, his love of fast cars *(Bullitt, Le Mans)*, of poker *(The Cincinnati Kid)*, of bikes *(On Any Sunday)*, of women (every movie), evident in each project he personally undertook. Bits and pieces of himself became his movies, perhaps more directly than in the case of any other movie star.

Yet in 1950 it had not yet occurred to McQueen that he might try acting. It took a girlfriend, of course, an actress, to introduce him to drama coach Sanford Meisner, who got him a two-line part in a Yiddish play, where Steve walked onto a stage, said "Nothing will help" in Yiddish, and departed. He did it eleven times a week for three weeks, and it made him enough money to pay one more month's rent.

It also set the course of his life: he was hooked on acting. He was astonished to find he wanted to study this bizarre craft in earnest. It was the most eager he had been to learn something new since discovering the joys of piston engines in the service.

And so, school-hating Steve actually enrolled himself with other fledglings at Meisner's Neighborhood Playhouse. It was a time when Steve was very happy, enchanted no doubt

with his ability to try on other people's faces for size. That was the main attraction. Pretending was a facet of the profession which tickled his childlike fancy, a memory echoing irresistibly from his youth, when all he wanted to do was get away with something.

He also liked meeting what he felt were free-thinking women of the still-Bohemian Village. Actresses, you know, urban, experienced. Smart cookies he could coax into after-hours rehearsals that lasted till morning.

Too, he made friends who stayed with him for life. There was one actress, for instance, Ellen Clark (now Hayers), who, like Steve, was a Meisner alumnus. "We did scenes together where you couldn't tell what was going to happen. He was always the most unpredictable person. One time he knocked me down to the ground in some scene, and nobody expected it, not him or me, and the whole class stood up, shocked. Steve just winked. That was his style. I don't know if any of us then thought he would make it, but when he did he never forgot us. I remember once, some time later, he had made it, and he was a star on TV in *'Wanted: Dead or Alive.'* I went to the set to visit someone else, and there Steve was. He saw me, stopped everything, and got me a part on the show. Just like that. He never forgot anyone."

McQueen went as far as he could with Meisner, but having exhausted the maestro's bag of tricks, he grew restless and wanted to move on. He found his next niche with the H-B Studios, where Uta Hagen and Herbert Berghof accepted him on scholarship under the GI Bill of Rights. Two years there and he moved on to the prestigious Actors' Studio, run by Lee Strasberg. He was one of five finalists selected from 2000 applicants. McQueen said later, "Nobody gives you talent. You either have it or you don't. What Lee gave me was definition."

But McQueen also would come to feel that much of his film career was in direct opposition to what he had learned at the feet of Meisner, Hagen, Berghof, and Strasberg. The guilt he felt in deserting the classical stage would manifest itself in his late-career insistence upon trying to do hard drama like Ibsen's *An Enemy of the People*. As if he had to apologize to his mentors for all those years he'd spent as the highest-paid movie actor of his generation.

For it really was acting that Steve discovered

he loved best of all the things he had done since leaving Chino, of all the things he could imagine yet doing. Accordingly, he committed himself to it.

He made the rounds of agents while appearing in summer stock, where his debut performance came with Margaret O'Brien in *Peg O' My Heart*, a piece of 1921 fluff restaged in upstate New York. He moved from there into national road companies, like *Time Out for Ginger*, with Melvyn Douglas, which toured following its Broadway run. He played in repertory with the Rochester Stock Company, doing *Member of the Wedding* with Ethel Waters. And then the break: replacing Ben Gazzara for three months in the drug drama *A Hatful of Rain*, Vivian Blaine his co-star. Ninety full days on Broadway! Then more: leading-man status playing Gary Merrill's

younger brother alongside Sam Jaffe in *Two Fingers of Pride* (alternately known as *The Gep*).

Theater—the perfect profession for Steve. He said: "Get to the theater between 7:30 and 8:00 at night. Finish by 11. No responsibilities. I love it." He was loved in return, with credits

His first 20 years are spent gathering the pieces of what will become his screen image. For example, the motorcyle—

16

—the racecar (a shot from *Le Mans*)—

—the gun (from *The Getaway*)—

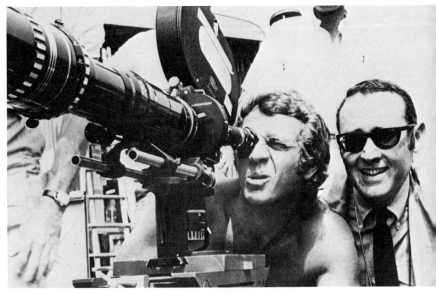

—and the movie camera.

Oh, yes: he also likes women. A lot.
Here, with first wife Neile Adams.
(Robert Perkins Photography)

With second wife Ali MacGraw. (Santiago Rodriguez)

and reputation beginning to build, in the press and in the industry. He was an actor.

Enter Neile Adams, the woman destined to be as important to him in his life as Nancy Sinatra Sr. was to Frank. The woman he would turn to for the rest of his life, even after they were no longer married.

Born in Manila of English and Spanish ancestry, which gave her a Eurasian cast with a gamine Shirley MacLaine appeal, she had been strictly raised by nuns. At 18 she saw dancing for the first time in a production of *The King and I,* and said, "That's for me." She fell wholeheartedly into the pursuit of the dance and became a scholarship student under the brilliant anthropology-influenced dancer Katherine Dunham.

She was a natural, like Steve. Upon graduation she replaced Carol Haney in *The Pajama Game* on Broadway and quickly became your basic toast of the town. She was rich, young, and pretty, and she dated the right people and she made the right newspaper columns.

One day she was on the arm of director Mark Rydell, who walked her into Downey's, kind of the struggling young actor's Lindy's, where he happened to see his buddy, budding actor Steve McQueen. Never the epicure, Steve was wolfing down a plate of pasta at a table by himself in the corner, his back to the wall as usual. Rydell introduced them as a matter of etiquette. But the moment meant more to Steve than Rydell was prepared for. As Steve remembered that turning point, "There was this dark tan skin and big white teeth, and she walked by in a tight skirt. I dropped a plate of spaghetti in my lap, just like in the movies." You can believe it verbatim. A week later they moved in together.

It was a period of adjustment and surprise for them both. While Steve had had move-in, move-out girlfriends before, he had never been stricken so hard. He threw himself full-weight into his first all-out courtship. "I showed her a way of life she never knew—the Village, the parties, not getting dressed up, no makeup, and going on long rides up in the hills. Man, it was real romantic." For Neile, the relationship was different from the start: "I had never been exposed to that type of man. I'd been brought up in convents, and suddenly this wild man was in my life. He made me feel very good and he made me feel very bad. He was honest, moral, and very protective."

What could these two have had in common? They shared, for one thing, the feeling of father figure deprivation. For Neile's father was an Englishman turned guerrilla in the war-torn Philippines, killed eventually by the Japanese. Consequently, Neile and her mother were incarcerated in a POW camp for the next three years, which Steve might have fancifully, if consolingly, likened to Chino. Then, too, they had a mutual love of things theatrical, though his was the world of the legitimate stage and hers of the musical. And, if nothing else, there is always the theory that opposites attract, for there could be no couple more unlikely than convent-schooled Neile Adams and reform-schooled Steve McQueen. Yet they were to stay together for 16 years.

But for now that is a millenium's distance into the far future. There is the immediate matter of supporting two people, not just one anymore, and that means extra work. Steve has heard that there is a Hollywood film crew in town, doing location shooting on the streets of New York. The word is out that they are casting extras, and it must pay because everyone in theater enviously and disparagingly knows what movie people make. If you care to sell out, that is. Steve is willing to find a buyer: no big deal. One fast shoot somewhere in lower Manhattan, not so far from the flat, really. And the chance for five seconds of immortality on a movie screen, for pay, is better than any scam Steve has cooking at the moment.

So he puts on his black leather jacket, kisses Neile goodbye, takes the stairs to the street three at a time, mounts his bike, and roars off in a cloud of blue exhaust, headed for the rest of his life.

With third wife Barbara Minty. (UPI)

19

Paul Newman in the true-life story of Rocky Graziano. Today he has barely any recollection of meeting the 26-year-old McQueen on the set. But McQueen remembered. (All pictures copyright © 1956 by Metro-Goldwyn-Mayer and Loew's Inc.)

Director Robert Wise insisted on authentic locations. Here, proud "parents" Newman and Pier Angeli (ironically the girlfriend of the late James Dean for whom the movie was written) make their way through a downtown Manhattan crowd, composed largely of non-professionals hired as atmosphere.

Somebody Up There Likes Me

MGM, 1956

CREDITS

Director, *Robert Wise;* producer, *Charles Schnee;* associate producer, *James E. Newcom;* screenplay, *Ernest Lehman,* from the autobiography of Rocky Graziano, written with *Rowland Barber;* photographer, *Joseph Ruttenberg* (b/w); editor, *Albert Akst;* art directors, *Cedric Gibbons, Malcolm Brown;* music, *Bronislau Kaper;* technical advisor, *Johnny Indrisano.*

CAST

Rocky Graziano *(Paul Newman),* Norma *(Pier Angeli),* Irving Cohen *(Everett Sloane),* Ma Barbella *(Eileen Heckart),* Romolo *(Sal Mineo),* Nick Barbella *(Harold J. Stone),* Benny *(Joseph Buloff),* Whiteley Himstein *(Sammy White),* Heldon *(Arch Johnson),* Questioner *(Robert Lieb),* Comm. Eddie Eagen *(Theodore Newton),* Frankie Preppo *(Robert Loggia),* Johnny Hyland *(Judson Pratt),* Lou Stillman *(Matt Crowley),* Announcers *(Harry Wismer, Sam Taub),* Uncredited bit player "Fido" *(STEVE MCQUEEN).*

Opened July 3, 1956 (110 minutes).

The world's first look at Steve McQueen: a shot, a slash, a scowl, a stare, a shrug, a smile.

Newman, still in the street punk stage of the script, fights off a car owner as the gang lifts hubcaps. McQueen is in the beret by the front tire.

REVIEWS

"Robert Wise's direction is fast, progressive, and bright, and the picture is edited to give it a tremendous crispness and pace" (Bosley Crowther, *New York Times).*
"A hard-biting movie and a good one. Its appeal is its basic honesty" (William K. Zinsser, *New York Herald Tribune).*

It is 1956. James Dean is dead. And it looks like Steve McQueen is going to get $19 a day just to stand around like a good extra. But he is able to parlay the part into some lines, even a close-up of his own, and that's going to pay him $50 instead of $19.

That's thanks to the director, Robert Wise, who spots this "kook in a beanie" and builds the part of Fido with him. Wise is a Val Lewton protégé risen from B-movie ranks to A-budget successes like *The Day the Earth Stood Still.* His talent for working with actors has not been submerged under the increased budgets, and Wise wields some power now. He has fought hard for these on-location day shoots around New York City, and he has won.

That is not the only battle Wise has fought on this picture. Originally written for James Dean, who has inconsiderately made a single

entity of his body, his Porsche, and a concrete bridge abutment, the film has gone through other actors' hands, including Montgomery Clift's, before arriving in Paul Newman's possession. There are fights about whether or not to go Method on this picture, and Wise wins here, too. The Manhattan-bred Method is In: people, by God, are supposed to become their parts.

The firm and feckless Wise follows his nose and his nose tells him that this McQueen character can handle it. So McQueen tries on the Method for size.

He's seen in the first 15 minutes of the picture, as a pool-playing punk who's part of young street hood Rocky's gang of petty thieves. Thick-haired with speech broadly inflected, he adopts pure Brooklynese, a foreign language to him, to anybody.

He appears first with his back to the camera, setting up a shot on a pool table. Touched suddenly from behind, he whirls around,

slashing the air with a switchblade that could not possibly have been in his hand a moment ago. It is a characteristic gesture; he'll use it again in *Baby, the Rain Must Fall.*

A few minutes into the movie, he's stealing hubcaps, robbing a fur truck, grabbing $20 suits off a fence's rack of stolen garments, fishing from rooftops through open windows to hook a radio, and slicing the air widely with his blade in a rumble. There is always a snarl on his face. McQueen plays it all like episodes from his own adolescence.

Wise, like McQueen a native of Indiana, likes the 26-year-old kid, but can't think how to use him again. The picture is over.

But eight years after this, Wise will pay superstar Steve McQueen a quarter million plus points to headline his roadshow block-buster *The Sand Pebbles.*

And nine years past that, producer Irwin Allen will offer ultrastar Steve McQueen $1 million flat, as an opening bid, to do *The*

Towering Inferno alongside and billed over Paul Newman, now his comrade in arms, the same Paul Newman he'd had a few scenes with in *Somebody Up There Likes Me,* when he was just a youngster, making that incredible $50 a day.

Another of McQueen's first screen moments, as he waits to hear his take in a fencing operation.

The victim subdued, the gang makes a break for it, with McQueen in what will become a characteristic catlike crouch, ready for an escape or a getaway.

McQueen is torn between the law and the crimes of his boyhood chum, racketeer John Drew Barrymore (seen right, son of The Great Profile and father of *ET*'s Drew). Singer Lita Milan looks concerned. (Copyright © 1958 by Allied Artists)

Never Love a Stranger

ALLIED ARTISTS, 1958

McQueen as bounty hunter Josh Randall, star and subject of CBS-TV's *Wanted: Dead or Alive.*

CREDITS

Director, *Robert Stevens;* producers, *Harold Robbins, Richard Day;* screenplay, *Robbins and Day, from Robbins' book;* photographer, *Lee Garmes (b/w);* editor, *Sidney Katz;* art director, *Leo Kerz;* music, *Raymond Scott.*

CAST

Frankie Kane *(John Drew Barrymore)*, Julie *(Lita Milan)*, "Silk" Fennelli *(Robert Bray)*, Martin Cabell *(STEVE McQUEEN)*, Moishe Moscowitz *(Salem Ludwig)*, Flix *(R. G. Armstrong)*, Brother Bernard *(Douglas Fletcher Rodgers)*, Bert *(Felice Orlandi).*

Opened July 9, 1958 (91 minutes).

REVIEWS

"Sincerely written and frankly fashioned. Shot in raw black-and-white that allows the documentary aspect of life to seep through the screen. But for all this, the film does not come to true life" (Richard W. Mason, *New York Times*).

"Rather unconvincing melee further confused by a pretentious narrative background filled with such mordant statements as 'Life is a span that links the eternities' " (Paul V. Beckley, *New York Herald Tribune).*

Completely by coincidence, Robert Wise calls up Neile one day and offers her a job. She takes it. But the decision is not without its trauma.

Doing the Metro film, *This Could Be the Night,* means moving at least temporarily and probably permanently to California. Steve likes New York. Besides, Wise has no idea of Neile's involvement with Steve; he has hired her simply because she is a dancer of note and he needs her in this semi-musical. He would have no use for McQueen in the picture, even if they came as a pair. Reluctantly, McQueen agrees to make the move, hoping that something, somewhere might come along for him, or for them. Even though he'll be 3000 miles from the stage, the place he calls home.

They set up housekeeping in a small motel across the street from MGM, but it soon becomes clear that Neile is the moneymaker in this family. That's hard for Steve to take: "He doesn't like the women in his family to have balls," his second wife Ali MacGraw will say, and it applies to Neile here and now. He is getting nowhere. He's made the rounds of agents, he's even willing to think about TV. But there are no takers.

Angry and despondent, he runs off on impulse with a couple of buddies, headed for bike-riding in Cuba. Neile is doggedly continuing the movie when one night the phone rings. It is Steve calling from Cuba: he's tired of running around, it's her he really wants, and will she marry him?

Yes.

As soon as he is back, they jump in the car and race off to wed. The rashness of the moment has its toll, though—nothing is open, and as Steve floors the accelerator to try to make the next J. P. before he closes, the speeding youngsters are stopped by two cops right outside San Clemente. But they are heart-of-gold cops. When Steve has explained the problem, they're taken to the local jail, where one of the patrolmen calls his minister, a Lutheran clergyman who's more than happy to meet them all at Mission San Juan Capistrano, where Steve and Neile long to exchange their vows. And so, with the two policemen as witnesses, they are married on November 2, 1956.

Their honeymoon is a week across the border in Mexico, for Neile has to be back at work on Monday.

Filled with fresh enthusiasm, Steve once again makes the obligatory appointments, and to his surprise finds that television wants him now. In fact, they're anxious for him. Television has become a free source of talent, a small-screen casting file, a tout for the big time, and McQueen has a new face on which someone is willing to take chances.

He picks up numerous guest spots, on the *U.S. Steel Hour, Armstrong Circle Theater, 20th Century-Fox Hour,* and a memorable part on the *Philco-Goodyear Hour* in "The Shrivington Raiders." On February 24 and March 4, 1957, he has a major role on CBS's *Studio One* two-part production of the Reginald Rose play *The Defender.* He plays the accused and is represented in the courtroom by E. G. Marshall, but it's a one-shot deal, and he doesn't go on to play anything else on the show that becomes *The Defenders.* But then he does get three days' work on producer Frank Gruber's *Wells Fargo* for a $400 fee. He is turned down in his bid to work steadily on the show because, he is told, at 5' 6" he is too short to be a Western hero. "Didn't anybody here see *Shane?*" he wonders, and consoles himself with fourth billing as "Rick" on *West Point.* CBS is beginning to look like home.

Plus, his agent's strategy to get his client movie work through TV exposure has worked. The movies want a piece of Steve McQueen.

In early 1958 he lands a supporting role as a District Attorney in Allied Artists' *Never Love a Stranger.* It is his first featured role in a motion picture. The studio, hunting for new, inexpensive, as yet unknown talent, thinks this TV kid is a good choice to play Martin Cabell, a Jewish lawyer stunned to find out that his childhood friend is not Catholic after all. This is played against a gangster background cooked up from the steamy mind of Harold Robbins, upon whose current best-seller this adaptation is based.

Though the movie is made by a studio that's halfway between poverty row and the majors, they've sunk a comparatively heavy $700,000 budget into making the picture. It is their first attempt to capture the best-seller market, which Robbins guards for himself by acting as producer and screenwriter for a $50,000 fee. Heavy money for a 1958 indie to put up front, but worth it, AA feels, because Robbins has already sold some 14 million copies of his books. Among them *A Stone For Danny Fisher,* which Paramount has bought, bleached, rewritten and retitled *King Creole* as a vehicle for Elvis Presley. Robbins wants to make damn sure that doesn't happen again, and retains control over the *Never Love a Stranger* property so that "the public would get the story as I wrote it."

McQueen does not like being away on location in St. Louis. The separation causes problems with Neile. "It was the one and only terrible part of our marriage," she has recalled. "We were thousands of miles apart. We didn't know each other very well and the minute we were separated, all the insecurities came flooding in." Their phone bill exceeded their rent payment, and more than one call ended with a slammed receiver.

But they must feel it's worth it. After all, her present income is ten times his, and they have to do what they can to help him retain his pride.

Allied Artists pushes the picture's release hard, opening it simultaneously at 75 metropolitan New York theaters, backed by an unprecedented $30,000 press budget. The film does well in the Northeastern urban areas, but its anti-anti-Semitic theme makes other exhibitors wary, and in New Orleans it is flatly refused a playdate. Similar obstacles arise in its subsequent European release. Though its florid, quasi-religious narration is a definite detriment, today the film is incredibly tame, and it's difficult to realize that as recently as 1958 the Ku Klux Klan would threaten to burn a Southern theater showing a movie portraying a favorable Jewish image.

Opening the film in July, 1958, is a mistake, too, for McQueen is just a few weeks short of his first nationwide fame. Had the picture been held up only another six weeks (certainly something nobody could have foreseen), it could have prominently featured his name in the ads, and come up a much more lucrative property for everyone, including Robbins and McQueen.

Because Steve McQueen has become a television star, seen by millions every Saturday night on CBS as the star of *Wanted: Dead or Alive.*

Earlier in the year, McQueen has guest-starred as bounty hunter Josh Randall on CBS's *Trackdown* series with Robert Culp. The appearance is a pilot for producer Vincent Fennelly, who has convinced the Four Star production company, headed by former actor Dick Powell, to introduce the character, to test his popularity and the potential for a fall spin-off series. Fennelly doesn't think McQueen's height will harm his chances to succeed as a generic hero. There may even be some sympathetic audience reaction when they see this little guy going up hard and heavy against the baddies. Indeed, feedback is positive and encouraging on the March 7, 1958, episode, and plans are set in motion to create a series around the Josh Randall character.

There are some problems. McQueen hates horses, and Four Star is intent on identifying Josh Randall with his horse Ringo, in tried and true western tradition. So, though McQueen retains his dislike, he trains daily on Ringo to the point where Four Star is confident enough to bring in PR people to do puff pieces on a boy and his horse.

It is an era in which a TV Western star is also identified by his weapon. There is Chuck Connors' rapid-fire piece on *The Rifleman,* *Yancy Derringer*'s titular armament, and *Wyatt Earp*'s extra-long Buntline Special. Accordingly, a buzzword gun is developed for McQueen. The props department, after obtaining the necessary legal sanction to alter a weapon beyond the law's restrictions, starts with a Model 92 Winchester lever-action rifle worth $1100. By the time they're through tinkering with it, this .44.40 has become a sawed-off, bob-tailed carbine more than illegal on any current American street but perfectly at home in the lawless old west. (The astute viewer, watching the shows in rerun, will note that the cartridge belt contains the larger and hence more impressive and photogenic .45.70 cartridge, of absolutely no use in the Model 92.)

McQueen works on his fast draw with his friend Sammy Davis, likewise a gun enthusiast, and the two of them spend Sunday afternoons in rapid-fire competition. When McQueen starts the practice, which he is told he must do if he is to be credible on the show, he needs considerable improvement. There are moments when it looks hopeless, as if he has hit his speed and that's it. But he applies himself to the task, steeling himself to be the best he can, and soon he is the equal of Davis, considered the fastest gun in Hollywood among weapons hobbyists.

Once proficient with the carbine, McQueen's confidence shows on camera, and just as Four Star had hoped, Josh Randall's "Mare's Leg" is the hook that captures the public and keeps them snared, week after week. The show, whether because of actor, horse, or gun, is an immediate success, and goes through two well-rated seasons, with McQueen becoming known as "the thinking man's cowboy," due no doubt to the program's sponsor, Viceroy, which calls itself "the thinking man's cigarette."

McQueen's salary goes to $100,000 a year, and he finally feels he's making enough to force Neile to give up her career. She does so willingly, her second thoughts many years away from this moment, and she devotes herself to being a full-time wife and soon-to-be mother.

Wanted: Dead or Alive will quickly rise and fall, though, when McQueen begins to exercise control over the scripts, honing them finely, trying to have the character emerge likeable,

heroic, yet still believable. The CBS executives retaliate against this young upstart by moving the show from Saturday to Wednesday, a graveyard slot against NBC's gangbusters *The Price is Right*. Ratings plummet from the once respectable, rent-paying 28.7 right down into the toilet, and the show will be canceled at the end of its third season, in May, 1961, after having racked up 117 episodes (still seen in syndication today).

But *Wanted: Dead or Alive* has made Steve McQueen's name a household word, and it has gotten him where he wanted to be.

He is taking it all real seriously. As race pal Denise McCluggage remembers, "He *had* made it. People in restaurants pointed at him and called him 'Josh,' and grinned those give-me-a-prize-for-recognizing-you grins. Steve rather stiffly reminded them, 'My name is Steve McQueen. The role I play is Josh.' "

Ever hungry, though, he is ready for more: "Now I don't have to lean on Josh Randall and his shotgun. I'm up for recognition now."

He is going to get it.

With actress Fay Spain in *Wanted: Dead or Alive.*

Producer Jack H. Harris trying again with the economical appeal of a double
feature, this time distributed in re-release by Allied Artists rather than Paramount.

The Blob

PARAMOUNT, 1958

CREDITS

Director, *Irvin S. Yeaworth, Jr.*; producer, *Jack H. Harris*; associate producer, *Russell Doughten*; screenplay, *Theodore Simonson, Kate Phillips*, from a story by *Irvine H. Millgate*; photographer, *Thomas Spalding* (DeLuxe Color); editor, *Alfred Hillman*; art directors, *William Jersey, Karl Karlson*; music, *Ralph Carmichael*; special effects, *Barton Sloane*; title song, *Burt Bacharach.*

CAST

Steve Andrews *(STEVEN McQUEEN)*, Jane Martin *(Aneta Corseaut)*, Police Lt. Dave *(Earl Rowe)*, Old Man *(Olin Howlin)*, Dr. Hallen *(Steven Chase)*, Sgt. Burt *(John Benson)*, Teenagers *(Robert Fields, James Bonnet, Anthony Franke, Molly Ann Bourne, Diane Tabben).*

LOCATIONS: Valley Forge, Pa.
A Tonylyn Production.
Opened September 12, 1958 (85 minutes).

REVIEWS

"If the acting is pretty terrible itself, there is becomingly not a single familiar face in the cast, headed by young Steven McQueen" (Howard Thompson, *New York Times*). "Aficionados of pseudo-scientific films will find 'The Blob' one of the best to come along in recent years. Not only does it have a monster with propensities that will curdle the dreams, but it is made with a stress on naturalism of behavior by the human beings who are menaced by the creature. The two qualities make the picture a minor classic in its field" (Paul V. Beckley, *New York Herald Tribune*).

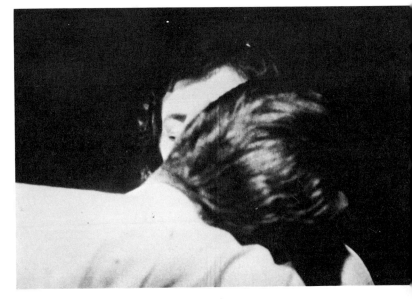

First scene in the movie is McQueen's entrance, suitably caught mid-smooch. Only the nearby landing of a meteorite disturbs his concentration. (All pictures copyright © 1958, Paramount Pictures Corporation)

All the kids his own age (28?) believe he saw the meteorite's arrival. Note the fact that McQueen is the epitome of the fifties teen hero, with his own girl and, more importantly, his own convertible.

First clue of the Blob's imminence is the disappearance of the town doctor. Of course, nobody believes the kids. Soon, though . . .

The Blob opens just as *Wanted: Dead or Alive* is debuting in prime time. It is a step backwards for McQueen's image, back to the teenage roles he thinks he's escaped with the Josh Randall character.

Nevertheless, it is today remembered as the film that not only gave the world man-eating Jello, but also the one that billed the actor, for the first and last time, as Steven McQueen. It is, additionally, the only movie where he plays a character named Steve.

The film comes at the height of a fast cycle of creature movies born, like the giant ants, spiders, and locusts, of atomic-based national anxiety. But *The Blob* is a little something different. It isn't a formula picture, though familiar elements creep in (e.g., people running through the streets in panic, that hoary shot of the tiny child right smack dab in the monster's path).

One reason it's different is that it isn't a studio picture. The producer is Philadelphia-based Jack H. Harris, who budgets this film at $240,000, the first in a series of similarly themed and marketed entries. He puts up $150,000 of his own money, so that when Paramount sees it, likes it, and buys it as an independent pickup for $300,000, his profit is an immediate, symmetrical 100 percent.

Paramount follows through with a tremendously expensive $300,000 ad campaign, which nets the studio $1.5 million in rentals the first month of release. Matching the negative cost with an all-out ad blitz sets a precedent, and a lucrative one at that.

This despite the fact that at age 28 McQueen is playing a high-schooler. Yet he is able to come across believably, and to insert certain elements which will come to belong to him. The movie begins with a full view of the back of his head (cf. the first shot in *Le Mans*), in a clinch on Lover's Lane. This, his first starring role, opens with a kiss and proceeds to delineate other facets of his persona, like his image as a loner who goes against peer group pressure and law enforcement authority to do what he thinks is right (cf. *An Enemy of the People*), as the adventurer who wants to know what's going on because he has to know (cf. *Bullitt*).

The lover, the loner, the hero. The McQueen image starts here.

Parts of the film still work quite well. It is the

definitive fifties film about the town that won't listen to the kids until it's too late. That moral is driven home by making the same age group that is watching the movie the subjects of the movie. The marketing strategy particularly resonates when the Blob comes oozing out of the projection booth on a Friday night when the theater is full of high school daters—exactly the crowd and on the night that would be watching *The Blob* in 1958.

Other moments of quality are delivered by the Blob itself. The special effects are quite nicely handled for a low-budget film (and most of the budget goes to animating the Blob—McQueen gets only $3000 for his role, after unwisely turning down a profit participation).

The picture also tries something interesting in its temporal and geographic structure.

Everything happens in a single night in one small town during darkness. The movie's running time is close to the time encompassed by the plot. And every moment of horror development is handled on its own terms, as the monstrosity mushrooms from one kid's discovery to an entire town's plight.

Elsewhere, though, *The Blob* is a mess. Adults are idiots, parents are deaf and callous fools, cops are worse. The dialogue is often less than senseless: "You mean that pebble's been hot-roddin' out in the stars?" or "Has everyone in this fool town gone crazy?" And there is an unforgettable moment as the high school principal wavers, letting all the laws of common decency stand between him and smashing a pane of glass to get to a CO_2 fire extinguisher to freeze the thing. Thank God he does.

Inevitably, the ever-growing, ever-glowing Blob takes on the town, imprisoning McQueen, Corseaut, and a diner owner's family beneath the gelatinous mass.

It takes 14 years to spawn a sequel: *Beware! the Blob* (aka *Son of Blob)*. The sequel is a cult item among college students for a while, but it dies, only to be reissued eight years after that, in 1980, on a double feature. It is oddly advertised as "The movie J.R. shot" because director Larry Hagman is rather centrally involved in the "Who shot J.R.?" mystery on TV's *Dallas.* The original *Blob,* second-featured, is mistakenly billed as "Steve McQueen's first film." It is, however, his first and last monster movie.

The moviehouse that is prime fodder for the march of the Blob.

32

The subject of the title, shot on location in Missouri, where McQueen was raised. (All pictures copyright © 1959, United Artists)

The Great St. Louis Bank Robbery

UNITED ARTISTS, 1959

CREDITS

Directors, *Charles Guggenheim, John Stix;* producer, *Guggenheim;* associate producer, screenplay, *Richard T. Heffron,* based on fact; photographer, *Victor Duncan* (b/w); editor, *Warren Adams;* music, *Bernardo Segall.*

CAST

George Fowler *(STEVE McQUEEN),* Gino *(David Clarke),* John Egan *(Graham Denton),* Ann (introducing *Molly McCarthy),* Willie *(James Dukas),* with men of the St. Louis Police Department in their actual roles in the original crime.

LOCATIONS: St. Louis.
SHOOTING TITLE: *The St. Louis Bank Robbery.*
Opened February 26, 1960 (86 minutes).
Re-released by Crystal Pictures, 1970.

REVIEWS

"The entire cast, excluding Steve McQueen, is unfamiliar, hence a freshness of faces. Likewise, the good photography and semi-documentary flavor of its actual St. Louis backgrounds. The pacing is far too slow and the neurotic clashes of the four thieves make the actual robbery anticlimactic and slightly absurd" (Howard Thompson, *New York Times).*

With the success of *Wanted: Dead or Alive* catapulting him into areas he has never dreamed of, McQueen finds himself in another movie, with his first above-the-title billing. It is the glum *The Great St. Louis Bank Robbery,* an independently produced film shot on location.

The picture seeks to reproduce in semi-documentary fashion the conception and execution of an actual crime. Most of the movie is wrapped up in planning and character development; only the last fourth is the robbery itself, based on a true incident. It is thus considerably unlike the prevailing tone of the current gangster pictures, mostly AA and AIP cheapjack flashes made strictly for the drive-in crowd.

Instead, it opts for authenticity, which is successful, and psychology, which is questionable.

The gang here includes David Clarke and Graham Denton. The film is the first time McQueen is allied on the screen with a gun, although TV viewers have been used to it for some time.

Typical of the darkness that permeates the film. Here, McQueen visits the college campus by night, musing over a milieu that has rejected him.

There is a girl, of course, played by the uninspired newcomer Molly McCarthy. Note his special approach to women: hands off, baby.

34

The timetable precision with which the crime is planned, the patient casings of which doors are locked, when peak banking hours are, how many seconds a red light takes to turn green—these details and their observation make much of the film interesting to watch.

But when it tries to go deeper, it becomes trashy. One of the four-member gang has seen his drunken mother fall down the stairs and die; another hides a strongly implied homosexuality; a third is shamed before his prissy sister. Here the film falls apart completely.

McQueen, star of the movie, is the driver of the getaway car. It is a fifties ideal: to be young, with wheels. His own real-life race-car image is descended directly from this kind of reel-life casting and role-fitting. At last McQueen is allowed to play his real age; he is a former college football player caught taking a bribe, the star athlete washed up and out who had gone to hide in the Army and who has come back now to his home town, and is reluctantly involved again with the girl he left behind.

All expressed in the gloomiest of terms. At one point, he returns to his old campus, wandering the expressionistically empty, shadowy stadium, where glory once was his; then he pines outside the frat house where long ago he knew friendship. Dismal.

Now he's a loner—essential McQueen stuff here—full of the burgeoning 1959 fear of Them: "They come around and They promise you everything. They keep you in college because you can do something well. They make you feel like you're God or something. One mistake and you find out you're just hired help."

At film's end, he lies on the bank floor, bleeding from a leg wound. The other three sprawl dead, victims of a technology they hadn't accounted for in their plans. He pleads, "I'm not one of them!", a quivering, apologetic mess. He cries. He cannot possibly be Steve McQueen.

The final quarter recreates the actual robbery, with McQueen at one point pointing his pistol right at the camera. That's semi-documentary.

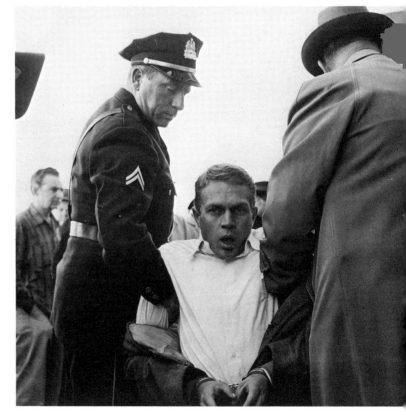

McQueen is the only one left alive at the end, and as he's dragged into the paddy wagon, he stares into space as the existential loner the script wants us to believe he is.

Never So Few

MGM, 1959

CREDITS

Director, *John Sturges;* producer, *Edmund Grainger;* screenplay, *Millard Kaufman,* from the novel by *Tom T. Chamales;* photographer, *William H. Daniels* (Metrocolor, CinemaScope); editor, *Ferris Webster;* art directors, *Hans Peters, Addison Hehr;* music, *Hugo Friedhofer;* gowns for Gina Lollobrigida, *Helen Rose.*

CAST

Capt. Tom C. Reynolds *(Frank Sinatra),* Carla Vesari *(Gina Lollobrigida),* Capt. Grey Travis *(Peter Lawford),* Sgt. Bill Ringa *(STEVE McQUEEN),* Capt. Danny de Mortimer *(Richard Johnson),* Nikko Regas *(Paul Henreid),* Gen. Sloane *(Brian Donlevy),* Sgt. Jim Norby *(Dean Jones),* Sgt. John Danforth *(Charles Bronson),* Nautaung *(Philip Ahn),* Col. Fred Parkson *(Robert Bray),* Margaret Fitch *(Kipp Hamilton),* Col. Reed *(John Hoyt),* Capt. Alofson *(Whit Bissell),* Mike Island *(Richard Lupino),* Billingsley *(Aki Aleong).*

LOCATIONS: Burma, Thailand, Ceylon, Hawaii. A Canterbury Production.
SHOOTING TITLE: *Sacred and Profane.*
Opened December 7, 1959 (124 minutes).

Publicity pose shot in the studio, emphasizing McQueen's action image with the ever-present gun.

Frank Sinatra, for whom McQueen has great awe and appreciation, sees new talent written all over the blond kid's kisser. (All pictures copyright © 1959 by Metro-Goldwyn-Mayer and Loew's Inc.)

REVIEWS

"It looks as though Frank Sinatra has been tapped to succeed Errol Flynn as the most fantastically romantic representation of the warrior breed on screen. John Sturges has directed it for kicks. Those who will get them are the youngsters who can be lightly carried away by the juvenile brashness of Mr. Sinatra, and by the swashbuckling antics of his pals, played almost beyond comprehension by Richard Johnson, Peter Lawford, and Steve McQueen" (Bosley Crowther, *New York Times*).
"Steve McQueen looks good as a brash, casual GI sergeant who overpowers two military policemen so neatly that Sinatra gets him transferred into his outfit. He may be better known to television viewers as the hero of 'Wanted: Dead or Alive,' but has appeared in such other films as 'Never Love a Stranger' and 'The Blob.' He possesses that combination of smooth-rough charm that suggests star possibilities (Paul V. Beckley, *New York Herald Tribune*).

McQueen's three small, independently financed features, coupled with his continuing weekly exposure on television, has accomplished exactly what his promoters have hoped for. His name and style are becoming increasingly widely known, and he has come to the attention of the majors. He is getting established, for just as Allied Artists had scouted the tube for fresh faces, so have the majors scoured the independent movies for new people. Someone at MGM thus sees Steve McQueen.

The picture the studio has him in mind for is *Never So Few*, the screen version of a best-selling WWII novel set in the Orient. It concerns Burma, in which 40,000 Japanese are kept at bay by 600 Kachin guerrillas led by a tough American captain, Frank Sinatra. MGM picks up the book while it is still in galley proofs, and, though the story is based on a *True* magazine story about actual events and real people, the studio thinks that the novel's fictionalized format will work very well for Sinatra and Gina Lollobrigida, the Italian star in her first American movie.

The original supporting cast is comprised of Peter Lawford, Richard Johnson, and Sammy Davis, but then Sinatra and Davis, prior to this the best of friends, have a spat and vow never

to work on the same set ever again. John Sturges, a renowned action director, has seen McQueen on TV in *Wanted: Dead or Alive*. Is his interest piqued because Josh Randall rides a horse named Ringo, nearly the same name as Ringa, the erstwhile Sammy Davis character? Or is it because he sees the young actor's possibilities? Whatever the reasons, he personally negotiates for McQueen's release from CBS to do the movie.

The role is fourth from the top, virtually a cameo or guest appearance, as a jeep driver, again associating McQueen's character with a vehicle he knows how to drive very well. Sturges is impressed with his work, to the point of seeing to it that McQueen receives a non-exclusive contract with MGM, allowing him to work outside the studio. So highly does McQueen regard Sturges's capabilities and understanding that the veteran director becomes a trusted guide and, ultimately, co-worker. They will work together immediately on *The Magnificent Seven*, then on *The Great Escape*, and they will attempt to mount a number of unmade films before turning to *Day of the Champion*, which will break up their long partnership as it very bloodily metamorphoses into *Le Mans*.

This is all in the future, however. For now, principal photography on *Never So Few* is taking place on the Metro lot, but it blends nicely with the actual location shooting, which MGM proudly touts in its ads. The truth is that only 10 percent of the film is shot in the Far East, with 40 percent done on Hawaiian sets to match the jungle shots in Burma and Ceylon. The remaining 50 percent is completed back in reliable old Hollywood, where there are no mosquitoes.

Never So Few opens at the end of 1959, to be eligible for Oscar nominations that do not come after all. It is quite a big picture for the year, and MGM thinks it's a very prestigious product, but its grandiose vision of war fares well with neither critics nor public. Harvard *Lampoon*, in fact, names it one of the ten worst movies of the year. McQueen, though, is singled out, especially by *Variety*, which ventures to say that the film should shoot him to stardom.

It is at this time that McQueen is also virtually adopted by Hedda Hopper, who says, "He excites. I took one look at that hardened face

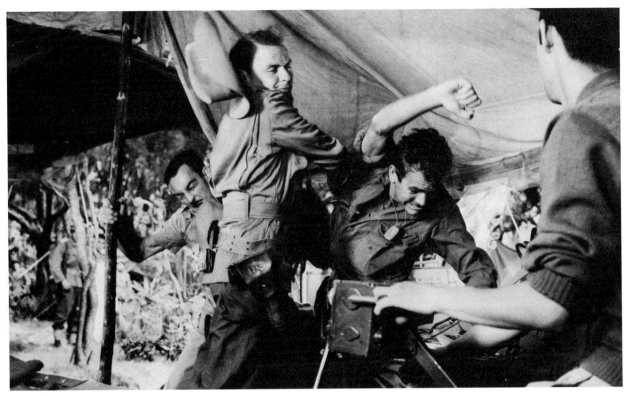

There are two sides to every Sinatra picture. This is one.

This is another.

39

A pair of public smiles off the set. Sinatra and McQueen form a mutual admiration society, but future picture plans will not jell.

and knew he had a past." Invited to her home for an interview and drinks, McQueen walks in demanding something to eat, and the usually unflappable Hopper serves him a piece of chocolate cake, undone by his straightforward approach. He winks at her and says, "Wanna ball?" and they are friends for life. He treats her like a chorus girl to her face, and she dotes on it, but as she is making his name increasingly well known through her columns, he refers to her out of her hearing as "a great lady." After her death, it takes her bereaved staff weeks to uncover the fact that all the unsigned, black-bordered tributes to her in the trade papers have been arranged anonymously by McQueen.

Of the associations McQueen makes on this, his first major role in an important feature, a significant one is made with Sinatra, who likes and admires the blossoming star's guts. He has that jive attitude Sinatra has always dug, giving interviews that sound like this: "Like, I'm playing a soldier in this picture, man. You might say it's a change from this Western thing I'm doing, right?" Scooby-dooby-doo, part two, thinks Sinatra. He proposes a deal with McQueen that he star in a project Sinatra has been eyeing to direct, the story of *The Execution of Private Slovik,* about the only soldier ever executed by the United States for treason. The project fails to come off because McQueen has too many commitments he does not know he has yet, but the story does become an acclaimed TV-movie in 1973, with Martin Sheen and without involvement by either Sinatra or McQueen.

McQueen has also met youthful Robert Relyea, *Never So Few*'s assistant director. Relyea will later become a McQueen confederate, serving as assistant director on *The Magnificent Seven,* assistant to the producer on *The Great Escape,* executive producer on *Bullitt, The Reivers,* and *Le Mans,* relative to his position at Solar, a company Steve is going to have to form for self-protection in four years.

But of all the people McQueen has met, it is John Sturges who will deal best with McQueen's cool strength.

In 1960, Steve breaks down and lets Neile act—but only with him. Here they are in the chilling "Human Interest Story" episode on TV's *Alfred Hitchcock Presents.* He'll do another one, "Man From the South," without her.

The Magnificent Seven

UNITED ARTISTS, 1960

CREDITS

Director, *John Sturges*; executive producer, *Walter Mirisch*; associate producer, *Lou Morheim*; screenplay, *William Roberts*, from original screenplay for *The Seven Samurai* (Japan, 1954); photographer, *Charles Lang, Jr.* (DeLuxe Color, Panavision); editor, *Ferris Webster*; art director, *Edward Fitzgerald*; music, *Elmer Bernstein*; costumes, *Bert Henrikson*.

CAST

Chris *(Yul Brynner)*, Chico (introducing *Horst Buchholz)*, Vin *(STEVE McQUEEN)*, Calvera *(Eli Wallach)*, Britt *(James Coburn)*, Bernardo O'Reilly *(Charles Bronson)*, Lee *(Robert Vaughn)*, Harry Luck *(Brad Dexter)*, Old Man *(Vladimir Sokoloff)*, Petra *(Rosenda Monteros)*.

LOCATIONS: Cuernavaca, Mexico.
A Mirisch-Alpha Production.
Opened October 23, 1960 (128 minutes).

REVIEWS

"A pallid, pretentious and overlong reflection of

Studio pose featuring the Seven: Coburn, Dexter, Vaughn, Bronson, Buchholz, McQueen, and Brynner. (All pictures copyright © 1960 by United Artists)

Brynner dominates the picture, as is his intent. He almost never removes his chapeau, for which a hatmakers' union cites him as the Hollywood actor who looks best wearing a hat. He survives to make the sequel.

McQueen, second in command, loves his role as Vin: "After a while you can call bartenders and faro dealers by their first name." He lives, riding off with Brynner at the end.

the Japanese original. Don't expect anything like the ice-cold suspense, the superb juxtaposition of revealing human vignettes, and especially the pile-driver tempo of the original 'Seven' " (Howard Thompson, *New York Times)*.

"The big screen is filled in a deeply satisfying manner. The battle is made up of the extravagant acrobatics, the leaps and dying falls which are the stuff of Western gun-battles. They are the ritual movements of the Western, as stylised as the Samurai, and should be accepted with as much respect" (Dilys Powell, *The London Sunday Times)*.

Never So Few has established McQueen as a supporting actor in the major studios' casting offices. But he has demonstrated more than a little potential, and for its new Western, now in pre-production, United Artists acquires him for a third-billed role as the quiet but deadly Vin.

UA has just this year begun to look like a major studio. Where once it had relied on the exclusive pick-up of pictures it had not produced, now UA is going into partnership with wily mogul Walter Mirisch. He is using UA as a distributor outlet for his glossy, expensive, handsomely packaged entertainments. Together with his brothers Harold and Marvin, Mirisch is on his way to becoming the most important and influential producing entity in Hollywood history. And his first big picture is *The Magnificent Seven,* based on Yul Brynner's idea that a Japanese film might be successfully translated into a Western milieu.

Mirisch has picked up the property from Japan's Toho Studios, whose 1954 feature *The Seven Samurai,* co-written and directed by Akira Kurosawa, has been seen in a severely truncated form in America throughout 1956 as the curiously retitled *The Magnificent Seven.* New York reviewers had noted even then that the material was rife with Western possibilities in its tale of warriors in feudal Japan who defend a village against a murderous overlord's band of marauders.

The subject matter is transformed literally yet liberally into a two-hour super-Western, replete with thunderous score, sweeping Panavision panoramas, and a cast of who's-who supporting actors. Today, any one of the film's major names would draw substantial box-office by himself.

Bronson, fully a decade away from his European-nurtured superstardom, in his second picture with McQueen. He dies, forever mourned by the village children.

Yet it very nearly does not make it onto the screen, facing almost insurmountable problems before it even starts to shoot. The Screen Actors Guild is threatening to strike, and there is question as to whether it will affect the shooting of *The Magnificent Seven.* But the project has been confirmed with contract signatures since July, 1959, long before the union's current dictate of January, 1960, and the movie is given the go-ahead to begin production in Mexico in February.

Whereupon actor Anthony Quinn files a $500,000 breach of contract suit against Yul Brynner, plus a $150,000 suit against UA, with whom he says he has acquired rights to film the Japanese screenplay. Brynner's attorney, Leon Kaplan, counter-claims that Quinn had given up his rights to be included in the film deal when he and Brynner could not come to terms. Quinn asserts that he should be compensated for his suggestions which are in the current script, but he loses his claim because there is nothing on paper anywhere that says he was ever involved.

And then Lou Morheim of Brynner's production company, Alciona, has declaratory rights relief action filed against him by Mirisch to counteract Morheim's claim that he has acted in a producer capacity and deserves such billing. Mirisch offers him ten weeks' salary at $1000 a week plus 5 percent profit participa-

Well-read Vaughn has not yet ventured into spyland with *The Man From UNCLE,* nor is he yet a Ph.D., but he will work with McQueen again in *Bullitt* and *The Towering Inferno.* He is shot in the back.

43

German heartthrob Horst Buchholz in his first American film, playing a Mexican would-be gunslinger. He stays behind with the girl.

Brad Dexter, #7 of the Seven, the one everybody forgets when they make bar bets. He doesn't make it either.

James Coburn *(left)*, still six years shy of his first starring role in *Our Man Flint*. Best friends with McQueen, they do *The Great Escape* and *Hell Is For Heroes*. He is killed. (Note the deep diagonal frame composition Sturges employs to give depth to the flattened wide screen.)

And the villain: Eli Wallach in a dry run for his role to come in *The Good, The Bad, and The Ugly* (he's the Bad).

—and shoot.

McQueen's two duties in the movie: brood—

tion in addition to the $28,000 he has already received from Alciona. Morheim refuses the offer, replies with a $600,000 cross-complaint, and finally receives his associate producer credit on the film.

All this before even a foot of film has rolled through the camera.

It is amazing that the picture ever does begin shooting. At least in Mexico it is a thousand miles away from the legal harangues. Everything runs smoothly. There are simply no

45

problems, and the picture finishes on time, and right on its rather high $2.7 million budget (which includes McQueen's $65,000 salary).

Some $800,000 has been earmarked for publicity, and the picture is sold in unusual fashion. For the first time, a major studio has adopted the multi-print saturation technique of distribution, heretofore reserved for low-budget exploitation features designed for quick play and fast pay-off. UA floods exhibitors across the country with hundreds of prints, keying its approach to the action-oriented South and Southwest, figuring that even for an A picture like this as much as 80 percent of its dates will be played off within three months of its premiere. Very good idea, very fast money: $11 million in America and Europe. On both sides of the Atlantic, it is regarded as an instant classic, and customers pay and pay again to immerse themselves in its tangy Western flavor.

Certainly the picture is not perfect. On the one hand, it's too clean: Eli Wallach, as a supposed Mexican bandit, walks around in what looks like designer jeans. Then, the script relies on easy psychology to explain each of the Seven's motivation in defending the village against the villains. Women are in the film only as prettified love interest or to serve the men in the cantina. Mexican actress Rosenda Monteros' ballyhooed American debut turns out to be only a nod in the direction of the Mexican government, and she's in the movie just to get a girl on the submarine, as they say. The rest of the Mexican actors, for the most part, do not play speaking roles. Those parts are taken by Hollywood actors, who fake the accent badly. And, technically, the inferior DeLuxe Color process has resulted in totally faded prints, so that the original color, which lasted two years at the most, is now just a memory.

But overall the picture still works remarkably well. As the most ambitious Western of the fifties, it is one of the first examples of the reflexive, or self-referential, American Westerns. It fascinatedly explores the roots of its own myth, and on that level, which director

Actual location shooting in Cuernavaca is impressive without being scenically overbearing, with the added benefit that it looks fresh and right: obviously not Topanga Canyon.

A cautious Brynner saddles McQueen with a shotgun so that nobody can outdraw him, but does not count on audiences connecting the weapon with McQueen's TV "Mare's Leg," drawing their attention back over to McQueen's side of the screen.

The essential goodness of the gunslingers is set at the very start when McQueen rides shotgun on a hearse Brynner has offered to rein to Boot Hill to bury an Indian nobody wants buried there.

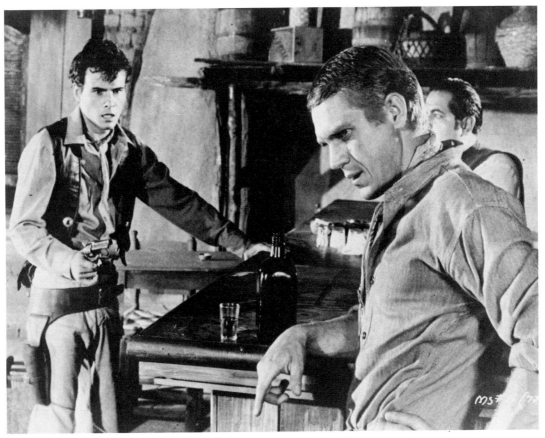

McQueen, as an aimless drifter content to tie down momentarily with anybody who needs him, is unperturbed by hotheaded greenhorn Buchholz's pistol act.

47

Sturges is fully aware of, and which is probably the reason he has made the film in the first place, *The Magnificent Seven* is a grand achievement.

For McQueen it is the solidification of his image as an American Western hero. He's seen the Japanese original, knows the hero bit backwards. But both he and Brynner realize that McQueen is playing the Toshiro Mifune second lead, the one that is remembered from the original. Just who did play the Brynner analog? Brynner jealously maintains his star status amidst the threat of the appealing supporting actors. McQueen, singled out because of his ever-increasing TV fame, rebels, saying, "When you work in a scene with Yul, you're supposed to stand perfectly still. I don't work that way."

It is also significant, in considering the construction of his image, that McQueen is the one who notices there aren't any girls in town when they first ride in. And he's the one guy who turns away from teaching the villagers how to shoot to catch a pretty face hiding among the trees. Later, he'll prove himself the most physically adept of the Seven, able to rein with either hand. And only he and Brynner will ride off at the end, suggesting a sequel.

There are, it turns out, three sequels, but none with McQueen. *Return of the Seven* (UA, 1966) again features Brynner as Chris, the Cajun gunfighter in black, the only character held over from the original. *Guns of the Magnificent Seven* (UA, 1969) stars George Kennedy as Chris, and bears little relationship to the first two movies. And *The Magnificent Seven Ride!* (UA, 1973) is a made-in-Europe eight-day quickie that puts the kibosh on the series for some time to come. Director Walter Hill's proposed big-budget sequel for Universal, co-written with Englishman Lukas Heller, has Walter Mirisch's participation but no part for Yul Brynner. Roger Corman's sci-fi remake, *Battle Beyond the Stars* (New World, 1980), is an interesting variation in that Robert Vaughn is cast as a world-weary space samurai, much like his part in the original.

McQueen, following this ultra-Western's enormous and unprecedented success, is now rarin' to become a movie star. He has guested with Neile on Perry Como's and Bob Hope's TV variety hours. Broadway is talking to him about a musical. He has to turn down offers. He has a house in Brentwood, a home in Palm Springs, 50 acres near Carmel.

MGM calls.

Dexter, McQueen, Coburn, Buchholz, and Brynner indulge in some offscreen cards and horseplay.

The Honeymoon Machine

MGM, 1961

CREDITS

Director, *Richard Thorpe;* producer, *Lawrence Weingarten;* screenplay, *George Wells, from the play The Golden Fleecing,* by *Lorenzo Semple;* photographer, *Joseph LaShelle* (Metrocolor, CinemaScope); editor, *Ben Lewis;* art directors, *George W. Davis, Preston Ames;* music, *Leigh Harline;* costumes, *Helen Rose.*

CAST

Lt. Fergie Howard *(STEVE McQUEEN),* Julie Fitch *(Brigid Bazlen),* Jason Eldridge *(Jim Hutton),* Pam Dunstan *(Paula Prentiss),* Adm. Fitch *(Dean Jagger),* Signalman Burford Taylor *(Jack Weston),* Lt. j.g. Beau Gilliam *(Jack Mullaney),* Casino inspector *(Marcel Hillaire).*

An Avon Production.
SHOOTING TITLE: *The Golden Fleecing.*
Opened July 10, 1961 (87 minutes).

REVIEWS

"A wild and labored operation" (Bosley Crowther, *New York Times*).

(Top) Full cast at attention: Lanteau, Bazlen, Jagger, Prentiss, Hutton, McQueen, Mullaney, Weston. (All pictures copyright © 1961 by Metro-Goldwyn-Mayer and Loew's Inc.)

(Bottom) The farce takes place in Venice, elaborately reconstructed in Hollywood. The only true outdoor shots are old grainy CinemaScope travelog footage used to establish location and to open up the play for the screen.

McQueen is the centerpiece, as a Navy lieutenant who uses a missile-tracking computer to predict the ball's fall on the roulette wheel.

Hutton and McQueen discuss the fine points of the scam.

The humor is nearly all physical, from slapstick (Hutton, Weston, and McQueen teetering on the ledge of their hotel)—

"In addition to indulging or encouraging Mr. McQueen, the director wasted the talents of several other actors in his concern for the obvious" (Joseph Morgenstern, *New York Herald Tribune*).

"It moves fast and easy and everyone in the cast seems to be enjoying it, and so does the audience. One can also say a good word for Jim Hutton and Steve McQueen, both of whom represent something new in Hollywood casting" (Archer Winsten, *New York Post*).

McQueen has now only to repeat the formula of his rise in the independent ranks with a similar feat in the majors. He wants a star part at a big studio.

He nearly gets it at United Artists, which offers him the lead as Dave the Dude in *Pocketful of Miracles* after Frank Sinatra and Dean Martin have both turned it down. While McQueen is on non-exclusive contract to MGM, which means he can be lent out on occasion, the studio nonetheless prefers him to stay close to home as they look for something for him to do. The part goes to Glenn Ford, who does it

—to sex schtick (the joke here is that Bazlen has to seduce McQueen, and she's the one who attacks first. How unlike him).

Women in the audience are beginning to wait for his trademark smile—

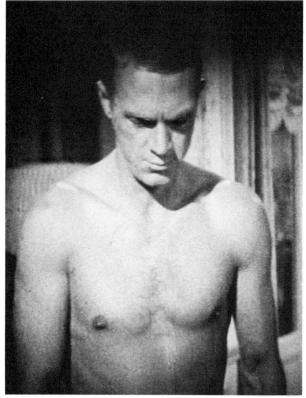

—and to catch a glimpse of him barechested, which is going to occur in practically every movie he makes from now on.

well, but it remains intriguing to imagine what McQueen could have done with a Runyonesque character in a period comedy.

MGM has been trying for some weeks now to secure Cary Grant for a part in its military comedy *The Golden Fleecing*, about a Navy man who uses the ship's computer to break the bank at a Venice casino. Grant, pretty much happily tied to Universal for the time being, is unavailable, so the studio begins to think about using the picture as a testing ground for McQueen's talents. In all his parts to date he has displayed a firm but easy touch which Metro feels might carry over into all-out comic farce.

McQueen himself is anxious to try his stuff. He suspects, vaguely, that comedy may not be his métier, or perhaps it is only this kind of comedy about which he feels uneasy. Either way, he finds he hasn't much to say in the matter because MGM, still exerting tight-fisted control over its properties, will make him do the picture whether he thinks he can handle it or not.

But Mother MGM knows best, right? It is one of the last of the grand old studios to maintain a talent development department, and McQueen is but one of a number of new actors the company is trying out in various vehicles.

Originally, the plan had been to make it an all-star production, from the moment MGM had bought rights to the source play, a Broadway comedy that turned out to be a flop long before its final performance number 84 at the Henry Miller Theater. Losing Cary Grant has been another blow. So the producers feel that the smartest thing that they can do right now is to use the movie version as a breaking-in tool for their nestlings. McQueen gets the Tom Poston role, Brigid Bazlen lands the Suzanne Pleshette part, Paula Prentiss does the Constance Ford character, and screenwriter George Wells fashions his script nearly verbatim from the Lorenzo Semple play, now retitled the sexier *Honeymoon Machine*.

McQueen seems ill-paired with Bazlen, lately Salome in Nicholas Ray's *King of Kings*. His life's history is explained away in a single line: "I still think if I'd gotten that bicycle for my thirteenth birthday, none of this would have happened." Her role, as the Admiral's daughter, is written to make her McQueen's verbal equal, but all she comes off as is a glamorous Navy brat on the make for a mate. At picture's end, she decides to capture McQueen by telling her father she's slept with the lieutenant—in ambiguous terms, of course, dating the movie more damningly than any other feature.

And there are plenty of elements to choose from. This Cold War comedy is overstuffed with icons of period paranoia: computers, missiles, Russians, Martians, spies, and fear of high technology. Still unwilling to face the terrors of atomic blackmail head-on, the movie buries the anxiety in comedy that makes Russians look like fools who slam tabletops with shoe heels. The subject can provide pointed film comedy, as witness this same year's *One Two*

The couple that does work in the movie, though, is Paula Prentiss and Jim Hutton, reteamed from *Where the Boys Are*. Their finely timed scenes together come off so well their work should be patented.

53

A typically brash moment with the Russians. How old-hat it all seems now.

Revolution! -twelve o'clock! · ·For Khrushchev's sake, what gives?????

Self-effacing, abashed, sheepish—none of these adjectives describes the McQueen of later films. Yet here he displays it all, in a dressing-down scene with Jagger.

Three by Billy Wilder, but MGM takes the easy way out, choosing to make a comic strip instead of an editorial cartoon.

To survive all of this, McQueen goes for broke, adopting a glib, smart-ass delivery, projected with snap, but enunciated and delivered so deliberately, so carefully, that every punch line is killed before it's out of his mouth. He relaxes only occasionally, and when he does you breathe a sigh of relief to see the real Steve, unfettered momentarily by his desperate defense, his rapid-fire tongue.

He generally gets very good reviews, however, and the film itself pulls in a few accolades for being a funny farce. But it is a genuine laugh factory antique now, something McQueen has perhaps presaged, confirming his feeling that he should have done anything to get out of the picture. He hates himself in it. He can't believe he's made a movie he hates more than *The Blob.* He's mad at the studio for making him do it and manages to get out of that non-exclusive contract which had seemed so precious to him just 18 months before. He will never go back to MGM again. Now he knows he will do things only on his own terms.

From that moment until he dies, that rule will not be broken.

Hell Is For Heroes

PARAMOUNT, 1962

CREDITS

Director, *Don Siegel;* producer, *Henry Blanke;* screenplay, *Robert Pirosh, Richard Carr,* from a story by *Pirosh;* photographer, *Harold Lipstein* (b/w); editor, *Howard Smith;* art directors, *Hal Pereira, Howard Richmond;* music, *Leonard Rosenman;* technical advisor, *Maj. William H. Harrigan.*

CAST

Pvt. Reese *(STEVE McQUEEN),* Pvt. J. J. Corby *(Bobby Darin),* Sgt. Pike *(Fess Parker),* Homer *(Nick Adams),* Pvt. James E. Driscoll *(Bob Newhart),* Sgt. Larkin *(Harry Guardino),* Cpl. Henshaw *(James Coburn),* Pvt. Kolinski *(Mike Kellin),* Capt. Loomis *(Joseph Hoover),* Pvt. Cumberly *(Bill Mullikin),* Sgt. Frazer *(L. Q. Jones),* Monique *(Michele Montau),* Capt. Mace *(Don Haggerty).*

LOCATIONS: California.
SHOOTING TITLES: *Separation Hill, The War Story.*
Opened June 26, 1962 (90 minutes).

REVIEWS

"An arresting performance by Steve McQueen, a young actor with presence and a keen sense

Director Don Siegel and cameraman Harold Lipstein get ready to shoot an interior. McQueen is just below the mike boom. (All pictures copyright © 1961 by Paramount Pictures Corporation)

of timing, is the outstanding feature. McQueen sharply outlines a provocative modern military type" (Eugene Archer, *New York Times*).

"Steve McQueen is extraordinarily good" *(New York Post)*.

"An unstintingly honest depiction of the hell of war. Among the more memorable men in the squad is Steve McQueen, whose word-at-a-time speech indicates an undercurrent of hostility" *(New York Daily News)*.

Steve McQueen's life is changing. He's got lots of money, he can take any part he wants for the asking, and he's got a family. His daughter Terri Leslie, born June 6, 1959, is two and a half; his son Chadwick Stephen, born December 28, 1960, is just over a year old now. Steve, Chad, Terri and Neile live in a $300,000 Brentwood estate once owned by actress Terry Moore. Everything is perfect.

That is all due in no small part to the fact that McQueen has firmly established himself in the public eye as a hero to believe in. Through *Wanted: Dead or Alive* and *The Magnificent*

Off the set with actors Adams and Darin, contemporaries of McQueen and often cast in the same mold.

Seven, he has become, to American audiences, the essence of the Western hero, the man of action who fights but on the side of right, who says little but who does much, who embodies certain cherished ideals nurtured in a century when life was easier to understand, when doing the right thing was the only thing to do.

To represent these sanctified ideas with his own rebel overlay is what McQueen has wanted to do all along—and he has, largely by instinct.

Now a trio of war films will cement those ideals, but on the battleground instead of the prairie. With *Hell Is for Heroes*, *The War Lover*, and most particularly *The Great Escape*, Steve McQueen will come to personify the fighting man and the national pride for which he stands. Defiantly, naturally.

McQueen is interested in a character named Reese in a script called *Separation Hill*, written by Robert Pirosh *(Battleground)*, who will also direct. Because it is a return to familiar WWII territory seen prior in *Never So Few*, in which

Adams, a year younger than McQueen, has likewise caught on with the public in a TV Western, *The Rebel*. But he fails to find the medium to propel him into movie stardom, as McQueen has, and he dies six years later in obscurity.

McQueen felt very comfortable, and because the character is written as a lone wolf who has learned to live by his rules and no one else's, he feels the role is tailor-made. It is as far removed from *The Honeymoon Machine* as he can get.

The picture, set in Germany in 1944, is the story of seven men who must hold a single position for two days while waiting for their company to return from reinforcing a squad in trouble some distance away. Based on a true incident, Pirosh has wanted to do the story since 1955, but it has taken seven years for the government to declassify the material. Pirosh pursues it until it is his, because it is a project that has grown from deep within himself.

But McQueen doesn't like pieces of the script. He wants Pirosh to change them, which Pirosh justifiably refuses to do. Upon which McQueen goes to Paramount and demands that Pirosh be replaced. By now McQueen actually has enough clout to pull this off, and Paramount sends Pirosh packing. It is an action which will become typical of McQueen, that he will enter a picture as the star around whom the film has been built, and then he will

Darin, at 25 the youngster in the cast, has made his name in records and in movies, but the heart condition that keeps him from full film fame will kill him 12 years later.

Newhart's screen debut. He does a version of the telephone routines he popularized on stage and records, as he delivers a diversionary tactic on a walkie-talkie to fool the enemy into thinking the seven-man band is larger than it really is. Seldom has a comedian's personal style been so neatly shoehorned into a script's demands.

An unattractive, grizzled McQueen begins his search for character roles with this film. Here he is pictured with an unidentified bit player in a scene cut from most prints.

Publicity still with Parker and Montau. No such scene appears in the movie.

take over. Never mind that he's only called the star: McQueen feels he must control the whole enterprise if it is to come off the way he wants it, which is to say correctly. More often than not he will prove to be right in his perceptions and subsequent demands, but a lot of heads roll along the way, and a defeated Pirosh's noggin is one of the first.

Don Siegel, a clever and hardy B-picture director, comes in on McQueen's approval, and together they revamp *Separation Hill* into *The War Story*. McQueen, however, doesn't think that's a very good title, either. He likes *Hell Is for Heroes*, which unfortunately is the name of another picture Paramount is concurrently shooting. McQueen McQueens-out all over the place and he gets the title he wants. The other movie, an Edmond O'Brien melodrama, becomes *The Soft Touch*, then *Deadlock*, then *Man Trap*, all so Steve can get his *Hell* out.

The victory does not mean that McQueen and Siegel get along. Reports drift in from the set that the two often quarrel violently, but no one is quite aware to what degree. As Siegel later recounts to Stuart Kaminsky, "McQueen walked around with the attitude that the burden of preserving the integrity of the picture was on his shoulders and all the rest of us were company men ready to sell out, grind out an inferior picture for a few bucks and the bosses. One day I told him that his attitude bored me, that I was as interested in the picture being good as he was, and that when this fact sunk through his thick head we would get along. I could see that he was angry. I knew that he was capable of violence and I knew he could whip me. So I decided that if he got up and came toward me, I would hit him first as hard as I could and hope for the best. Fortunately, he didn't get up. Eventually, we grew to like each other."

The motion picture *Hell Is for Heroes* comes out good, in spite of its tangled lineage, because it concentrates on individual and cooperative ingenuity rather than huge battle scenes. It decries military obedience and discipline, surely one of McQueen's most recognizable influences on the script, and praises the creative survival tactics of a small group of men under fire. They try to outsmart the enemy rather than outshoot them. One man's loss, says the movie, is the removal of a thinking obstacle between the squad and death at the hands of the advancing Germans.

As a kind of dry run for the next year's all-male *Great Escape, Hell Is for Heroes* boasts extraordinary achievements on a very limited budget. There is so little money, in truth, that at one instance McQueen finds himself defending foreclosure on the cameras. He draws a circle in the sand around the cameras with a stick and declares, "Anyone who steps over that line gets the shit knocked out of him." He stuffs his customary two pieces of Juicy Fruit into his mouth and stands his ground. The picture continues, economizing by shooting scenes on repeat sets carefully altered to hide the belt-tightening.

The cast, though, is the thing, like *The Magnificent Seven* a roster of interesting faces and accomplished support. The script's seven-man structure works even better than a similar one for *The Magnificent Seven*, and at least as well as the one coming up for *The Great Escape*.

Siegel's direction is tight and understated, and he has managed to work in his constant theme of the outcast under McQueen's nose. He doesn't allow the noise of the usual war movie to interfere with his small study of

Neile, Steve, and Adams on the buffet line one evening after a long day's shoot. The nearby California locations made it easy for Neile to visit the set regularly.

Siegel tries to work on the shooting script as Darin inveigles him into a fast game of chess.

59

bravery and ingenuity under pressure. Instead, the dialogue, largely retained from the original Pirosh script, is almost laconic, so that when battle sounds do come and when men do die screaming, agonizing deaths that really let you know what it's like to be shot and know you're dying, then has Siegel made his point.

So has McQueen, top-billed over the title as the clear star. His entrance into the film, though, is not a star's entrance, but unobtrusive, like any ordinary guy. Tight-lipped, cool, and lean, he lights like a cat, joining the company and immediately defining himself by his refusal to take orders. He mutters only monosyllables, but with a quiet, bitter intensity that accentuates his aloneness. He is a private throughout the film, busted from master sergeant, testimony to McQueen's consistent image as a defiant non-conformist to whom authority means nothing. That rejection of authority is redeemed in the film, and in McQueen's own life, by a highly moral set of personal standards which will not be broken, and which, in the movie, leads to his character's death as he sacrifices himself by rolling into a pillbox with a bomb, saving the platoon. The company salutes him with a funeral pyre by flamethrower.

Despite the picture's estimable achievements, Paramount throws it away as a double feature with *Escape from Zahrain*, another film of which the studio thinks nothing. It is shown at neighborhood theaters, without benefit of showcase, then it quietly vanishes, doomed to endless reruns on the late show. Only when the French critics discover American directors, putting tough little action-master Siegel in vogue, does its status increase.

A pity, for it is an earnest film, so earnest that President John F. Kennedy spoke the filmed foreword that preceded the film in its theater dates (a prologue now excised from TV prints). But even that star of stars could not bring box-office luster to a film that wouldn't give in to convention.

Like McQueen himself.

Exterior of one of the actual Boeing B-17 Flying Fortresses, completely refurbished and made air-worthy for the film.

The War Lover

COLUMBIA, 1962

CREDITS

Director, *Philip Leacock;* producer, *Arthur Hornblow, Jr.;* screenplay, *Howard Koch,* from the novel by *John Hersey;* photographer, *Bob Huke* (b/w); aerial photographers, *Ron Taylor, Skeets Kelly;* editor, *Gordon Hales;* art director, *Bill Andrews;* music, *Richard Addinsell;* costumes, *Elsa Fennell;* general technical advisor, *Lt. Col. Robert F. Spence,* USAF; Flying Fortress technical advisor *Lt. Col. William Tesla,* USAF.

CAST

Capt. Buzz Rickson *(STEVE McQUEEN),* Lt. Ed Bolland *(Robert Wagner),* Daphne Caldwell *(Shirley Anne Field),* Marty Lynch *(Gary Cockrell),* Junior Sailen *(Michael Crawford),* Singer *(Viera).*

LOCATIONS: Bovingdon Air Field, Manston Air Field, Cambridge England.
INTERIORS: Shepperton Studios, England.
Made with the cooperation of the USAF, the 3rd USAF in Europe, and the Royal Air Force.
Opened October 25, 1962 (105 minutes).

Co-pilot Wagner and pilot McQueen at the controls. (All pictures copyright © 1962 by Columbia Pictures)

REVIEWS

"Goes to remarkable trouble to avoid what it is talking about. One would have thought Steve McQueen ideal for the title role, and he might have been so, had he been imaginatively used" (Richard L. Coe, *The Washington Post).*

So enthused with military procedure is McQueen after the completion of *Hell Is for Heroes* that this former Marine private gladly

61

The studio wanted an American girl doing an English accent. They got English actress Shirley Anne Field instead.

McQueen conquers Field with smooth talking and a hard, mean kiss, just for the kick of stealing her away from best buddy Wagner.

narrates and stars in a 30-minute documentary for the public relations wing of the Marine Corps.

Then an offer to do a film called *The War Lover* in England brings added incentive, beyond its $75,000 fee and its reinforcement of McQueen's tough-American-hero image: It puts him right next to the famous and challenging Brand's Hatch race track.

It has become obvious to both Neile and the Hollywood crowd that Steve's great love is not movies, not even women, but anything that runs by internal combustion. He has been tooling around with bikes for over a decade, and dozens of cars have passed in and out of his life. He likes to do more than tinker, though: He has found he is a race-car driver at heart. "Speed is incredible and beautiful," he explains to family and company, and whenever he gets the chance he runs out and does 130 mph someplace, just to relax.

The Brand's Hatch race track, regarded as the center of British racing, is fascinating to him, and it is the major reason for him to do this English film, the only one he will ever

An obligatory behind-the-wheel scene for obsessive driver McQueen, Wagner at right.

make. It marvels him that his acting and racing lives will be able to co-exist within only a few kilometers of each other.

While in the UK, he decides to live in high style at last, and moves into the ritzy Savoy Hotel. Soon he is kicked out for using an illegal hot plate in his room, which sets the curtains on fire, resulting in his running through the hall in his skivvies searching for a fire extinguisher.

With imported family at his side, he takes up residence in a three-story Knightsbridge townhouse, rented from Lord John Russell for $1200 a month. It is a mansion so lavish that all production meetings are held there for sheer comfort's sake. The luxury is not lost on Steve, but the lure of burning rubber is stronger, and he leaves the home base often to visit Brand's Hatch, while preparations for shooting the 1943-44 war drama are being handled by the staff.

During his sojourns to the track, essential pieces of production design are under way. There will be no miniatures utilized for the film, and all planes will be rebuilt from the

McQueen turns his guileless mystique inside out to become a cold-blooded psychopath whose savage interior is hidden by this smiling mask.

63

ground up for actual flight capability. Columbia hires Capt. John Crewdson of the RAF, who resurrects three Boeing B-17 Flying Fortresses for the picture, dragging them out of the dirt they had lain under for a decade outside Dallas, Texas, and transporting them the 5000 miles to the RAF base at Bovingdon, England, to be readied for the skies once again.

The special work is undertaken by Aviation Services, Ltd., which was born when Alfred Hitchcock needed someone to rig up the technical angles of a helicopter chase for *To Catch a Thief.* Even as Capt. Crewdson flight-readies the mammoth prop-driven Fortresses, he is retiring the refurbished Tiger Moths and Fokkers he has just rebuilt for *Lawrence of Arabia.*

As Crewdson tightens piston rings and checks altimeter accuracy, technicians are busy elsewhere at Bovingdon, and at Manston RAF Base as well, converting the look of 1962 into that of 1943 for location shooting on the grounds. Bovingdon, one of the main B-17 centers during the war, is redressed and messed up for the film. Its clean designs are covered in dirt, its buildings sided with corrugated aluminum to simulate makeshift Nissen huts.

McQueen is surprised upon his return to commence principal photography that his risk-neck penchant for racing has become so well known that the producers have protected themselves in case of his injury or death. A company has insured Columbia to the extent

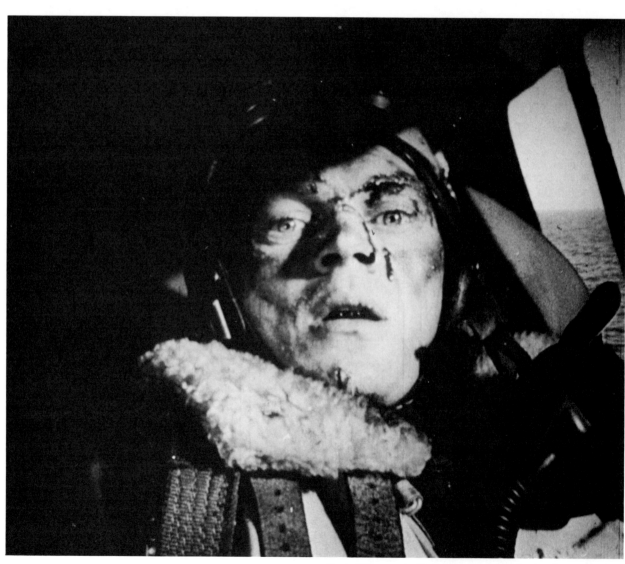

End of the movie: McQueen, alone in the fatally crippled Fortress, sees the end coming and goes down with his ship.

that were he hurt or incapacitated during the filming, he would be sued for $2½ million, the cost of the picture. Columbia forbids him to touch a race car before shooting is over, and they back it up with a clause in his contract. He has no choice but to give in.

In a sense he is complimented, because he has arrived at the point where a movie cannot be made without him. But his primary reason for coming to England, to play on the race track, has been taken away from him, and he is one teed-off movie star. Neile is relieved, however; now she knows he'll live through the making of the movie. When he starts an engine, she never knows . . .

So McQueen goes for the part. The role is Capt. Buzz Rickson, a man who takes orgasmic delight in flight. So strong is his need for war that he ignores orders, subjects his crew to unnecessary dangers, and parades his defiance like a banner. His eyes widen in thrall when he first enters his plane, a Flying Fortress with a cartoon of a woman dropping bombs painted on its fuselage. Sex and death are one. He flouts authority ("Rules are for sergeants") and flaunts his hot-shot irresponsibility.

Paired against him is his more humanitarian co-pilot, Robert Wagner, an underestimated actor whose good looks have been both his meal ticket and his limitation. His part directly counters McQueen's: Wagner is the man who lives for life, McQueen the man who lives for death. Their juxtaposition as foils is one of the good points of the film. So is the crisp monochrome photography.

But in sum the film is a failure. The dialogue is awful. It insists on spelling out in full paragraphs what an audience could grasp intuitively. Its heavy-handed explanations are insulting, like the flight surgeon's tell-all, "Captain Rickson is an example of the thin line that separates the hero from the psychopath." Just in case you don't get it. Later he says, "I consider war a complete negation of rational behavior." Who doesn't? Worst of all is McQueen's cry to the skies, "When you come up with a bomb big enough to blow up Rickson, you can blow up the world!" Bomb is right.

Nevertheless, McQueen is quite good and it is his picture. He is completely convincing in deed, if not in word, as a man who finds the sight of machine gun tracers more beautiful than the dawn they're fired into. His essential aloneness is best communicated by his eloquent non-verbal gestures. From the moment he sits up in bed in his star entrance to the last five minutes as he fights to save a failing Fortress, he knows what he's doing. He even gets moments to reinforce his persona, like wildly driving a jeep to an on-looker's appreciative, "No one in the whole 8th Air Force drives a car like Buzz!"

Most interesting about his performance, however, is the fact that he uses his charm and his smile against himself to turn out a portrait of a war-mad looney, modulating his easygoing manner into a tense viciousness concealed behind tightly drawn features. His face—face-filling McQueen grin and all—is a mask. He is a perfect son-of-a-bitch.

The escape is carried out on two fronts. Here, the POW's man a tunnel-in-progress. (All pictures copyright © 1963 by United Artists and Mirisch-Alpha).

The Great Escape

UNITED ARTISTS, 1963

That's Bronson in charge of scouting out what lies ahead.

CREDITS

Producer-director, *John Sturges;* assistant to producer, *Robert Relyea;* screenplay, *James Clavell, W. R. Burnett,* from the novel by *Paul Brickhill;* photographer, *Daniel L. Fapp* (DeLuxe Color, Panavision); editor, *Ferris Webster;* art director, *Fernando Carrere;* music, *Elmer Bernstein;* costumes, *Bert Henrikson;* casting, *Stalmaster-Lister;* technical advisor, *C. Wallace Floody, MBE.*

CAST

Capt. Virgil Hilts/The Cooler King *(STEVE McQUEEN)*, Bob Hendley/The Scrounger *(James Garner)*, Squadron Leader Roger Bartlett/Big X *(Richard Attenborough)*, Ramsey/The SBO *(James Donald)*, Danny Velinski/The Tunnel King *(Charles Bronson)*, Colin Blythe/The Forger *(Donald Pleasence)*, Louie Sedgwick/The Manufacturer *(James Coburn)*, Willie *(John Leyton)*, Flt. Lt. MacDonald/Intelligence *(Gordon Jackson)*, Eric Ashley-Pitt/Disposal *(David McCallum)*, Cavendish/The Surveyor *(Nigel Stock)*, Sorren *(William Russell)*, Ives/The Mole *(Angus Lennie)*, Nimmo *(Tom Adams)*.

Longtime friends Garner, McQueen, and Coburn have some laughs off the set.

LOCATIONS: Germany.
A Mirisch-Alpha Production.
A British Company Picture.
SHOOTING TITLE: *The Last Escape.*
Opened August 7, 1963 (168 minutes).

REVIEWS

"A first-rate adventure film, fascinating in its detail, suspenseful in its plot, stirring in its climax and excellent in performance. Steve McQueen plays a familiar American war-movie type—brash, self-interested, super-brave emoter. For sheer bravura, whether he's pounding a baseball in his catcher's mitt in solitary or stumping cross-country on a motorcycle with scores of Germans in pursuit, Steve McQueen takes the honors" (Judith Crist, *New York Herald Tribune*).

"There's Steve McQueen, surly and sophomoric, tediously whacking a baseball into a glove, one of the most moronic running gags in years. The film grinds out its tormenting story without a peek beneath the surface of any man, without a real sense of human involvement. It's strictly a mechanical adventure with make-believe men" (Bosley Crowther, *New York Times*).

The other job is the conversion of this prisoner (MacCallum)—

—into this disguised escapee. The transformation is carried out a hundredfold as the plan reaches fruition.

The Fourth of July celebration, a fictional element added to appeal to American audiences.

An infraction of the rules leads one to the brig, known here as the cooler. It is a locale familiar to McQueen from his stint in the Marines.

At first he doesn't know what to do.

But he has his catcher's mitt—

And here we are finally at the picture that gives Steve McQueen what he has wanted from the beginning: With *The Great Escape*, he becomes a movie star. Peculiarly, it is not his best picture, though it is marvelous in its own right. It is not his own favorite. It doesn't portray what he would've done in the same situation, finding Hilts's resignation to the confines of the cooler a bit too acquiescent for his own liking. He doesn't even like the business with the catcher's mitt. But everything

—and that seems to do the trick.

There's that smile again.

comes together for him in this one as it never has before.

McQueen goes into the film for many reasons. For one, while in England he has bought TV rights to *Beauty and the Beast.* This unlikely project fails to coalesce once he is back in the States, and perhaps for good reason. Then, he has been turned down for the lead in *Period of Adjustment,* which is awarded instead to Tony Franciosa. Doesn't matter: he'd have had to work at MGM, which he'd rather not do.

He has, however, been offered $100,000 to do this scrumptious part on location in Germany, a war drama with comic elements about—well, a great escape. Set to direct is John Sturges, who worked with McQueen on *Never So Few* and *The Magnificent Seven.* Once he hears Sturges is involved, McQueen jumps. He makes just one demand of Sturges: He wants his role to conclude with a dazzling cycle chase across the German countryside, Nazis breathing down his exhaust every kilometer of the way. Sturges agrees, although such an occurrence is not in the original, actual escape upon which the movie is based.

The plot comes from the details of Paul Brickhill's fictionalized treatment of the escape. That daring run took place in 1944 in Stalag Luft III, the prisoners organized by Roger Bushnell, known in the novel and film as Roger Bartlett (Richard Attenborough). The

escape attempts themselves were led by George Harsh, a pardoned killer who didn't make it out of the camp, but who did live through the war and considerably beyond, until 1978, when he died of natural causes in Toronto. The McQueen role is roughly analogous to Harsh's part in the escape. (Harsh and Bushnell's plans were so successful, incidentally, that millions of German troops were deployed in pursuit of the escapees. In the end, only three made it to safety, 50 were executed outright, and 26 more were returned to high-security camps to wait out the war.)

As McQueen makes the film, he finds it the culmination of his desire to put pieces of his life on the screen and thereby create an image for himself. The stuntwork, the defiance he is allowed to show, the humor with which he deals with authority, all flow from himself into the movie. He learns something new from Sturges, how to react rather than merely to act. He figures out all of a sudden how to let the camera do the acting for him. From this picture on, his acting style changes radically, and affects the rest of his career.

Prior to staging the lengthy bike sequence, McQueen goes over the moves with director Sturges.

70

The scene starts with McQueen noticing he's trapped between the Germans and two large barbed-wire barriers.

Between the two, he chooses the barbed-wire.

He makes the first barrier . . .

. . . but the second barrier is impossibly high, and McQueen tries to skid under it.

He can't get through the coils of wire and falls to a crashing halt.

Bloody but unbowed he has no choice but to surrender.

And so Capt. Virgil Hilts, the Cooler King, is returned to Stalag Luft III.

The result is that, as always, he takes command of the moviemaking. Warhorse writer W. R. Burnett *(Little Caesar, High Sierra, The Asphalt Jungle)* has been brought in to add some American characters to an otherwise all-British cast. He combines Harsh and McQueen and invents a part for James Garner, and adds bits of warmth along the way. Among his contributions are the discovery of the tunnel named "Tom" and the Fourth of July celebration. But the scope of his work changes dramatically when McQueen himself enters the picture. "McQueen was an impossible bastard," Burnett growls later. "A third of the way through the picture McQueen took charge. I had to rewrite his scenes and rearrange them. Ohhh, he drove you crazy."

Nobody—not McQueen, Sturges, Mirisch, or UA—is the slightest bit concerned that two other escape films are at the same moment being readied for release. One is Andrew Stone's British-made *The Password Is Cour-* *age* with Dirk Bogarde; the other is Jean Renoir's perceptive French *The Elusive Corporal.* Whatever their merits, and they are many, Sturges's approach will outstrip them on the single merit of size. At nearly three hours long, his will be the largest film of its kind ever made.

It is because McQueen, Sturges, Mirisch, and UA are involved, along with James Coburn and Charles Bronson, that *The Great Escape* bears an askance resemblance to *The Magnificent Seven.* But while the Western's accent was on action, this war drama concentrates on process.

And it is that process—the deucedly clever setting-up of the escape with what is at hand, and no more—that is the picture's great virtue. Cooperation, as in *Hell Is for Heroes,* is what is important: a tailor converts uniforms subtly and carefully into street clothes; a bird watcher uses his lectures to cover up briefing sessions; a forger manufactures false identity papers; a

73

Steve shows Neile part of his new gun collection he has acquired as an investment.

glee club leader chooses to practice Christmas carols that have the same rhythmical structure as the sound of tools tunneling under the floor beneath the choir's feet.

McQueen watches all of this construction with an eagle eye. He has no time to return to the States to see his family, so he installs Neile, Chad, and Terri in a Munich chalet just a stone's throw from location shooting at Geiselgasteig.

As he enters his part, he adopts a likeable, careless delivery as a pilot who already has eight escapes to his credit. He's a former chemical engineering student who, in one of Burnett's cursed rewrites, had supported himself with "bike-riding, flat trucks, county fairs, picked up a buck here and there." McQueen looks right at home in sweatshirt, chinos, leather jacket and duffel bag. No better command of body language can be found in any of his films. Always abjuring long speeches, he prefers light, quick sentences, and, if possible, expression and character development in the use of his body alone. If he's in close-up, he'd rather react than act now,

74

McQueen constantly practices his riding off the set, only to find some of his work has already been doubled for him.

The *Life* magazine cover, July 12, 1963. (Photos copyright © 1963 by John Dominis. Reproduced by permission)

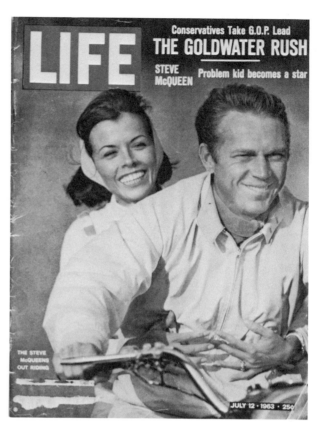

Life: McQueen presents a scholarship award at his alma mater, Boys Republic at Chino.

Life: In his old room at Chino, now graduated to counselor.

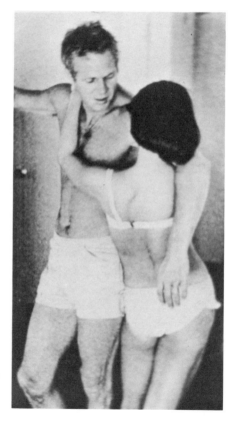

Life: With Neile in Palm Springs.

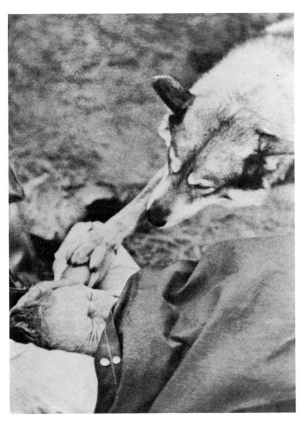

Life: Camping with his dog Mike.

Life: Out with the boys.

thanks to Sturges's advice. *The Great Escape* offers him ample opportunity to develop judiciously chosen gestures as emblems of an intense inner tension just aching to spring through that smiling, unruffleable exterior.

One of the most recognizable McQueen set-pieces in his quarter-century career comes near the end of this film: It's simply the best individual bike work ever put on screen, Hell's Angels epics included—and Val Kilmer's near-perfect parody in Zucker/Abraham/Zucker's *Top Secret* excluded.

There had been a time when Sturges had assumed he would have to shoot the entire picture in the United States, doubling Big Bear park for Germany. But his better sense prevailed and the whole movie has been made in Germany after all. Nowhere is that decision better appreciated than in this bike sequence, with Panavision wide-screen cameras capturing the full sweep of the mountainous West German locations. There is actually little spectacular stuntwork in the scene, only a single jump, really. But McQueen's sunny survivalist determination to be free couples with Sturges's visual know-how and split-

second editing make the sequence truly thrilling.

McQueen does all his own riding except for the much-too-dangerous 60-foot hurdle over the barbed-wire fence. That is doubled for him by his lifelong friend Bud Ekins. He even plays double himself at another point during the chase: Through a little camera manipulation, McQueen, alternating between the Hilts costume and a German solider's uniform, is able to chase himself because his "pursuer"'s face is carefully hidden. But it is McQueen on both bikes, getting paid to risk his life on wheels before the cameras. A far cry from the leash Columbia kept him on during *The War Lover.*

He smiles. *The Great Escape* is turning into everything he wanted.

He even makes the cover of *Life* magazine, with Neile gamely smiling as she rides tandem behind him on his cycle. When *The Great Escape* opens a month later, everyone suddenly knows Steve McQueen.

When first offered the picture, he is already contemplating doing Carl Foreman's *The Victor* (without the final "s" as yet), because it will be his third war movie in a row and because he

77

Life: After a bike session.

Life: Taking a sulphur bath with Neile.

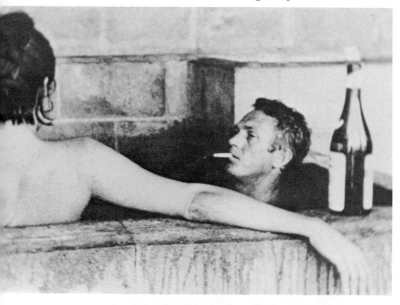

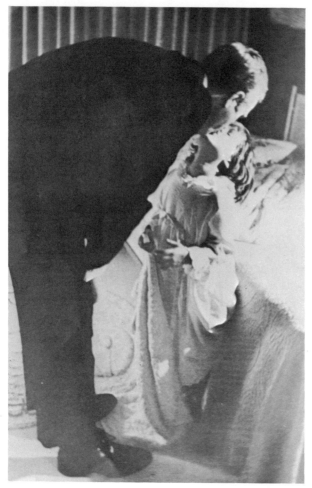

Life: Kissing Terri good-night.

78

can work with Sophia Loren, Ingrid Bergman, and Simone Signoret. He hesitates; he can only do one or the other. His instinct, which is the center of his being, tells him to stick with Sturges. His instinct proves correct. None of that glamorous cast makes it into *The Victors*, which opens and closes to poor notices and bad box-office.

His judgment is further confirmed by the glowing reviews from the London premiere of *The Great Escape,* two months before its scheduled American bow. That most of the POW's in the actual camp were Canadian and British has inspired the English promoters to go all the way to salute Sturges's monument to their countrymen's heroism. Sturges is made a Friend of the RAF, the highest civilian honor possible. And on the day of the premiere, five RAF bands parade in front of the Strand Theatre while jets buzz it overhead.

Eight weeks of European word-of-mouth excite the American audiences to a frenzy, so that when the picture does open in New York it is a hands-down financial success. Honors are heaped upon the movie, not the least of which is its being named Best Picture of the Year by the Madras, India, Parents' Association.

With the rewards comes Steve McQueen, movie star.

(Opposite page) The best portrait of Steve McQueen ever taken. (Photo: John Dominis).

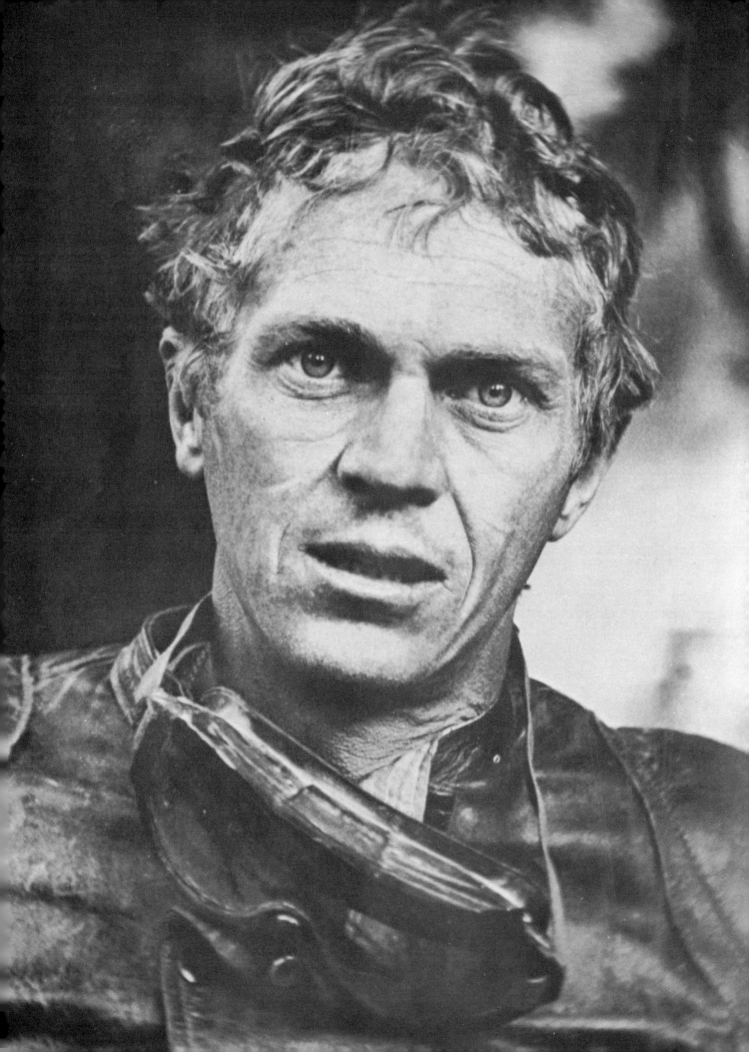

Hence the title. The scene is actually at the very end of the movie, as it is in the book. (All pictures copyright © 1963 by Allied Artists Pictures Corporation)

Soldier in the Rain

ALLIED ARTISTS, 1963

CREDITS

Director, *Ralph Nelson;* producer, *Martin Jurow;* associate producer, *Dick Crockett;* screenplay, *Maurice Richlin, Blake Edwards,* from the novel by *William Goldman;* photographer, *Philip Lathrop* (b/w); editor, *Ralph Winters;* art director, *Phil Barber;* music, *Henry Mancini;* costumes, *Jerry Alpert, Shirlee Strahm.*

CAST

M/Sgt Maxwell Slaughter *(Jackie Gleason),* Supply Sgt. Eustis Clay *(STEVE McQUEEN),* Bobby Jo Pepperdine *(Tuesday Weld),* Pfc. Jerry Meltzer *(Tony Bill),* Lt. Magee *(Tom Poston),* MP Sgt. Priest *(Ed Nelson),* MP Sgt. Lenahan *(Lew Gallo),* Chief of Police *(Paul Hartman),* Frances McCoy *(Chris Noel),* Capt. Blekeley *(Adam West).*

Opened November 27, 1963 (87 minutes).

REVIEWS

"McQueen is simply callow with his striking of foolish attitudes, his butchering of the English

WHAT A TEAM!

Two terrific stars...in the wildly wonderful story of a pair of sergeants who leave the peace-time army in pieces! The million-dollar schemes they dared, the fabulous dolls they shared...and that little island they had stashed away in the Pacific...where everything tilted up, especially the girls!

Bobby Jo Pepperdine ...not exactly in the army, but she's really "with it"!!!

ALLIED ARTISTS Presents

JACKIE GLEASON & STEVE McQUEEN

A BLAKE EDWARDS PRODUCTION

Soldier IN THE RAIN

Co-Starring TUESDAY WELD · TONY BILL · TOM POSTON · ED NELSON

MUSIC – HENRY MANCINI

Produced by MARTIN JUROW · Directed by RALPH NELSON
Screenplay by MAURICE RICHLIN and BLAKE EDWARDS

So sure is McQueen that Gleason is the right man for the part that he foregoes top billing and waits until Gleason finishes shooting his CBS-TV variety series to get the picture rolling.

language, and his sporting of hick costumes" (Bosley Crowther, *New York Times*).

"McQueen, one of the more exciting actors around, is totally suppressed as a mush-mouthed stupid devoted to dawg and buddy to the point of tears" (Judith Crist, *New York Herald Tribune*).

"McQueen, with phony accent, jumps around as if he had ants in his pants, overdoing it so much that I could hardly recognize the fine comedian of 'The Great Escape' and 'The Honeymoon Machine' " (Wanda Hale, *New York Daily News*).

"Should set back his blossoming career one giant step" (Archer Winsten, *New York Post*).

With Steve McQueen, movie star, come the rewards. He has a healthy bank account, a

A publicity still featuring the co-stars, pushed in press releases as a twist on the Gable/Tracy, McLaglen/Lowe tradition by pairing two opposites. Said with a straight face.

81

Ed Nelson and Lew Gallo play McQueen's nemeses.

shelf full of racing trophies, homes in Palm Springs and Brentwood. He can command $300,000 a movie on the strength of *The Great Escape,* and he has to find something to do with all that loot. He hires a business manager, who tells him to invest, invest, invest. He buys a fabulous gun collection. Not enough, the business manager tells him, so he also acquires a percentage in a couple of restaurants. Some land, of course. A bowling alley. A Los Angeles office building. And a Christmas stocking factory.

Suddenly it isn't all cars, movies, and family anymore. It's business, which Steve knows nothing about. But remember? He didn't know how to ride a horse or draw a gun for *Wanted: Dead or Alive,* and see how good he got? He is about to do the same trick, but in the business world. He is sure of his future and applies himself to learning how to make more money. There is no such thing as too much.

The privacy he has always guarded so aggressively now begins to slide from his control. One night he has to hold a prowler at bay with a 9mm Mauser from his collection. The man tells police, "All I wanted was refuge and piece of mind. I am a good judge of character and

thought this guy would understand me, as I have seen many of his movies." There is no danger, it turns out, but McQueen is beginning to realize the consequences of fame.

There are, of course, compensations. He's a hot property now, and he and John Sturges talk about doing a romantic comedy, *Vivacious Lady.* But McQueen is preoccupied with his own protection as a viable and valuable Hollywood commodity, and he resurrects his old company Solar, named for his house at 2419 Solar Drive in Nichols Canyon, where his children had been born. He looks upon that time as idyllic, and perhaps by using the Solar name he can bring back some of that more innocent time.

Solar had begun as a safeguard enterprise which McQueen didn't really know how to use back in 1961. Today, as he scouts properties, he comes to the understanding that to make films his way he must also function as the producer, albeit uncredited so that to one accuses him of producing films as a testimonial to himself. He is to produce independently, then go into partnership with a studio distributor, entitling him to both a salary from Solar and a profit participation in the picture through the studio. He is thus able to collect from both ends.

Unfortunately, the first picture released under the Solar aegis is a bomb, a lackluster farce made from William Goldman's rather compassionate 1960 novel. There is every reason to think that the picture will succeed in the beginning. While it is in no way a war movie, it is still a military continuation of several themes espoused in *Hell Is for Heroes, The War Lover,* and *The Great Escape,* his last three projects. He has returned to his first home, Allied Artists, where he is installed in Gary Cooper's old dressing room. And the property itself, acquired in 1962, tells the endearing story of the oddball, bittersweet, often slapstick relationship between a fatherly master sergeant and the lusty, cornball supply sergeant he befriends, all spoken in Goldman's ear-catching dialogue.

Everything seems to be going right with the casting of Gleason and Tuesday Weld, and the film is set for popular director Blake Edwards, whose *Breakfast at Tiffany's* and *Days of Wine and Roses* are among the day's top films. But Ralph Nelson is guiding Sidney Poitier to an

Oscar for *Lilies of the Field,* and McQueen thinks Nelson is one of the few directors who could make the novel's actionless humor cinematic while retaining its integrity as a parable of friendship and male-bonding.

He is wrong. The picture is a disaster. Part of the failure surely lies in its timing, for it is released five days after the assassination of President John F. Kennedy. Even so, some lines would never be funny: to wit, Gleason's confession that he is a narcissist (!), whereupon a wide-eyed McQueen answers, "I thought you was as crazy about girls as anyone else." The whole movie is like that. And even in more sexist times, who could get away with the declaration, "I rate women the way schoolteachers mark tests, A,B,C,D,F, and incomplete."

McQueen also goes in too far over his head. He so broadly overplays his part that he comes off like Gomer Pyle with a permanent adolescent erection. His ideas of humor is to use his

Check out these wildly overdone facial expressions to understand why McQueen hates himself in comedy.

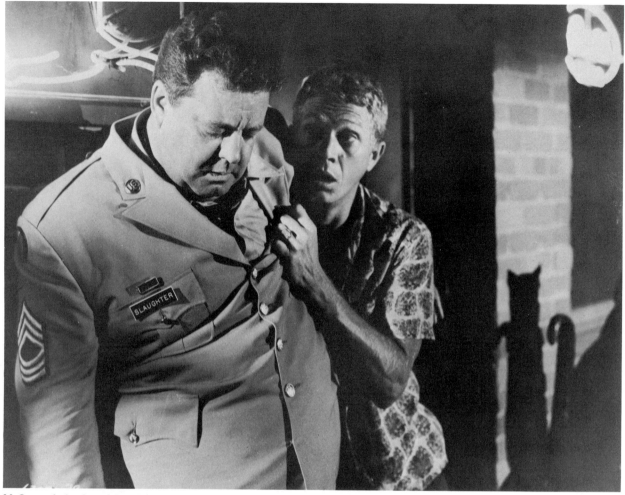

McQueen helps his idol and father figure out of a bar after they've just beaten up two MP's.

jaw like a shovel. Gleason, though, is quite good, fitting his bulk into the part as if it were custom-made. Surprisingly quiet, he doesn't fall back on his Poor Soul character to make it through. He acts with feeling and sincerity. The difference between the two men is that Gleason lets it happen while McQueen forces it, so totally wrong for the part is he.

The women in the movie have interesting roles, though. Tuesday Weld, in the book a 14-year-old Southern Lolita, is aged a bit to make her legal. Her introduction comes in an auto collision with McQueen's convertible; her first duty is to adjust her lipstick in the askew rearview mirror. Chris Noel has a subsidiary part, but it worth noting that at one point in her career she was known as "The Method Body."

Still, McQueen doesn't get the girl in this one. All he gets is bad reviews. So he vows never again to tackle comedy. He's been burned, and now he's going to be more careful about the movies he does.

Off the set, McQueen poses for yet another camera.

Love With the Proper Stranger

Paramount, 1963

CREDITS

Director, *Robert Mulligan;* producer, *Alan J. Pakula;* screenplay, *Arnold Schulman;* photographer, *Milton Krasner* (b/w); editor, *Aaron Stell;* art directors, *Hal Pereira, Roland Anderson;* music, *Elmer Bernstein;* costumes, *Edith Head.*

CAST

Angela Rossini *(Natalie Wood),* Rocky Papasano *(STEVE McQUEEN),* Barbara Margolis *(Edie Adams),* Dominick Rossini *(Herschel Bernardi),* Anthony Columbo (introducing *Tom Bosley),* Julio *(Harvey Lembeck),* Mama Rossini *(Penny Santon),* Marge *(Arlene Golonka),* Accountant *(Richard Dysart),* Cye *(Vic Tayback).*

LOCATIONS: New York City.
A Boardwalk-Rona Production.
Opened December 25, 1963 (100 minutes).

REVIEWS

"He's a face-squinching simpleton, for my money" (Bosley Crowther, *New York Times*).

Wood and McQueen in a publicity pose unrelated to the film. (All pictures copyright © 1963 by Paramount Pictures Corporation)

"McQueen does not strike one as belonging too successfully to this Italian family" (Archer Winsten, *New York Post*).
"McQueen is more mannered under Mulligan than he has ever been before" (Andrew Sarris, *Village Voice*).
"Fresh, funny, and endearing. The performance that catches the eye in Steve McQueen's, mainly because it's so busy. In relaxed moments, however, he does act with real charm" (Philip Oakes, *London Sunday Telegraph*).

The ads for the movie say, "There is a moment—a long moment—when everything is risked with the proper stranger." McQueen's new stranger is director Robert Mulligan, to whom he is going to entrust a new phase of his career: Steve McQueen as contemporary youth

McQueen strikes his stance as a jazz musician with That Look in his eyes. Even the unlit cigarette dangles at the correct angle.

The lair of the smarmy abortionist smacks of Caligari.

Mulligan visually emphasizes the distance between people.

That popcorn-selling, theater-filling, studio-rent-paying kiss.

Note the mouse. Got it from Wood's brother Herschel Bernardi. Deserved it.

The picture is filled with accomplished character actors, including Tom Bosley in a charming, unassuming movie debut as Wood's hesitant suitor.

in modern setting, with no wars or Western skies to back him up. For the first time since leaving the stage seven years before, McQueen is going to carry a vehicle entirely through acting.

Mulligan, with producer partner Alan Pakula, are overnight Hollywood heavies, thanks to the three Academy Awards their *To Kill a Mockingbird* has just won. The search for a hot follow-up property comes to a halt when they have found Arnold Schulman's screenplay for *Love With the Proper Stranger.* Schulman, a successful Broadway playwright of some renown whose *A Hole in the Head* is already a regional theater perennial and whose *Jennie* is currently playing. Pakula particularly feels that a Schulman script will bring the production the prestige it requires. A class dramatic product consciously molded to be Oscar-worthy from the beginning is what the team is after.

The story Schulman gives them is about a nice Italian girl who discovers she's pregnant by the not-so-nice Italian boy she's been seeing. Their relationship is explored, for the most part, on a single Sunday afternoon which will include a trip to the abortionist. Whether she will go through with it is one of the conflicts in the drama, as is the question of how much love is involved in the matter.

Pakula and Mulligan had breached the rape silence daringly yet inoffensively, even Oscar-winningly, in *Mockingbird,* and they hope to do the same with the abortion question in *Stranger.* The treatment is a touchy subject, because the operation is illegal everywhere in the United States, and taking a stand on it might be considered both chancey and laudable.

It is Pakula who has the knack for casting, and he suggests Wood and McQueen for the parts. Now getting Wood is no problem. Her presence in the picture almost guarantees critical acclaim because she has received two Oscar nominations for *Rebel Without a Cause,* and *Splendor in the Grass,* actors' dreams all. The challenge of this new role is appealing, the third time could be the charm, and signing her is simple. McQueen, however, has to fight for the part since he is not the first choice: Paul Newman has been mentioned as a leading character, particularly because he has played Italians on screen before. But once McQueen has convinced Mulligan of his ability, his credentials, and his sincerity, he gets the role and places his fate in Mulligan's hands.

As the rewrites take shape, the picture begins to look more like a comedy-drama overlain with a glossy Americanized neo-realism, filmed on the streets of New York, which McQueen approves—after all, it's where he got his start under Robert Wise. Pakula and Mulligan want it downbeat, no matter what, and this is what attracts McQueen the most. He knows from Sturges's lessons on *The Great Escape* that less is more, and that his greatest strengths lie in his smallest movements. This part gives him a superb chance to underplay and to gain thereby the professional actor's standing he is so determined to achieve. He's tired of publicity puff photos showing him doing the Watusi with Luci Baines Johnson, or whatever. He wants Sandy, Uta, Herbert, and Lee to be proud of him. He wants to grow up.

Therefore, doing an adult drama about love and abortion in the big black-and-white city seems perfect to him. Inevitably, the film will not quite live up to his expectations. The abortion doesn't take place, expectedly, because Wood freaks out at the last minute, so as not to offend the Catholics in the audience. So people go into the theatre hoping to see a sensationalistic star-heavy soap about abortion, but leave thinking about love.

The perfecting of love is the film's real subject: "Love that is mature, not just erotic or romantic, is an art," says a minor character,

On the streets of Manhattan with McQueen, producer Pakula, Wood, director Mulligan.

At the end of the movie, the camera pulls back from this Macy's streetcorner to show us that Wood and McQueen are just two of the millions of stories in this naked city. McQueen is barely discernible in the center of this final shot.

89

"and like any art it requires practice, concentration, consistent dedication." Thematically, then, the film is worthy.

But Wood and McQueen don't act as if they're in love. Plus, they are just plain flat wrong for the parts. She doesn't quite convince as the sister of a Lower East Side fruit seller, she just isn't made for this slice of life about New York blue collars, with roots in *Marty* and *The Catered Affair.* McQueen, though honest and straightforward in his part, is about as Italian as Sammy Davis. Together, they look like they're slumming.

On the positive side, the narrative does raise some fascinating points. McQueen is for the first time pitted against a single adversary, who turns out to be a woman. And a woman who is allowed to sleep with men for the same reason men sleep with women: sex and sex alone. It's a surprisingly advanced idea, for it treats women as men's equals, even to allowing them the same sexual rights. Wood's role is quite nicely written, with hardly an anti-feminine moment in it. Her character is her own woman, and McQueen's difficulty in dealing with her on that basis forms the most interesting facet of the picture.

But when the movie turns from a story of everyday people into a romance, roughly halfway through, the mood suddenly softens and the story treatment tenderizes. Piano music on the soundtrack takes the place of the first half's street noises, dissolves replace high-key cuts, and the film begins to embrace more of the conventions of the Hollywood romance. You know—mush.

Mush notwithstanding, the movie garners five Oscar nominations, as planned. But it is a year dominated by the English *(Tom Jones)* and the extinct *(Cleopatra).* Schulman's story and script nomination lose improbably to *How The West Was Won;* art direction goes to *America, America;* Milton Krasner understandably relinquishes his hopes to James Wong Howe's *Hud;* the costume award is given to *8½;* and Natalie Wood's third nomination becomes Patricia Neal's prize for *Hud.*

And though no less a publication than *Newsweek* has championed McQueen to win Best Actor, he is not even nominated.

Baby, the Rain Must Fall

COLUMBIA, 1965

CREDITS

Director, *Robert Mulligan;* producer, *Alan J. Pakula;* screenplay, *Horton Foote,* from his play *The Traveling Lady,* produced on Broadway by The Playwrights Company; photographer, *Ernest Laszlo* (b/w); editor, *Aaron Stell;* art director, *Roland Anderson;* music, *Elmer Bernstein;* technical advisor, *Billy Strange.*

CAST

Georgette Price Thomas *(Lee Remick),* Henry Thomas *(STEVE McQUEEN),* Deputy Slim *(Don Murray),* Judge Ewing *(Paul Fix),* Mrs. Ewing *(Josephine Hutchinson),* Miss Clara *(Ruth White).*

LOCATIONS: Bay City, Texas.
A Park Place-Solar Production.
SHOOTING TITLES: *The Traveling Lady,*
   Highway.
Opened January 12, 1965 (93 minutes).

REVIEWS

"Few films have come so total a cropper under such fine auspices" (Judith Crist, *New York Herald Tribune).*

As in *Love With the Proper Stranger,* director Robert Mulligan's emphasis is again on visualizing the distances between people. (All pictures copyright © 1965 by Columbia Pictures).

"A picture that tries hard, accomplishes much, and ends on one of those downbeats that leaves you unsatisfied" (Archer Winsten, *New York Post).* "McQueen, a fine comedian with a disarming smile, wasn't chicken when he took the part of poor Henry, sad sack, ill-fated, emotionally immature. This vital actor just isn't the type to portray such a long-suffering fellow" (Wanda Hale, *New York Daily News).*

Despite *Love With the Proper Stranger*'s commercial success, its lack of personal rewards—or awards—disturbs McQueen greatly, for he had pinned a lot of serious ambition on its acceptance. He all but retires from film, and it will be two years before he'll make another movie.

In the meantime, he has once again decided that cars, not movies, are his life. His personal collection has included a Jaguar, a Mini-Cooper, a Land Rover, a VW, a Lincoln, a Triumph, and any number of Ferraris, one of which he publicly cries over when he totals it. There follows an endless procession of Porsches, customized dune buggies, a Cobra (most of which will come to be sold at a 500-

piece public auction in November 1984, four years after his death).

He bike-races a lot and, finally, in September, 1964, part of Neile's worst nightmares come true. Steve is a member of the U.S. cycle team in the International Six-Day Trials in Germany. As he rounds a lap, a spectator suddenly jaywalks onto the track and McQueen swerves to avoid him, crashing his Triumph through the guardrail, bringing a stunned audience to its collective feet at once. Mother of mercy, is this the end of Terence Stephen McQueen? No—but the accident injures his leg, lays his

A few months before his accident, McQueen, in tails yet, makes his only Academy Awards appearance to present the Sound Achievement Oscar with Claudia Cardinale to *My Fair Lady*.

cheek open to the bone, splits his mouth wide, and knocks two teeth clean out. Not to mention two kneecaps which no longer have any skin on them. Within hours he is under the care of Europe's most accomplished plastic surgeons.

In France, soon thereafter, he is named the country's most popular foreign actor, and the adulation he receives is overwhelming. Aided by DeGaulle's personal makeup man, he has to hide his kisser under a moustache and goatee so he can walk through the Paris streets freely. But he is also covering his scars under the disguise, secretly fearful that he will lose his public if they find out he has been marked permanently by the wreck. He has never been vain, only religious about his daily two-hour physical routine of calisthenics he has designed for himself to tone both muscle and reflex, which he considers equal and correlated. But they will do his face no good, and as much as he hates admitting it, he knows his face is his fortune. So he keeps his mending physiognomy off the microscopically cruel movie screen until every last vestige of injury has vanished. His control of the media is so powerful that neither press nor public ever hears about any of this.

It is Robert Mulligan and Alan Pakula who drag McQueen out of his paranoid retirement to coax him into a role he seems born to play. Together with screenwriter Horton Foote, an Oscar winner for the Pakula-Mulligan *To Kill a Mockingbird*, they have adapted Foote's 1954 play *The Traveling Lady* for the screen. Mulligan has always been attracted to Foote's vision of life at the rural level, a naturalism without rutting and squalor. The complexities of the inarticulate are his concern and his forte, and, predictably, McQueen goes for his work in a big way. Foote's ability to portray the low-keyed in print provides the framework that an actor of limited but effective range, like McQueen, can build on. The raising of an eyebrow in Foote is equivalent to a half-page of declamatory speech in other writers. And McQueen hates to talk.

Mulligan, who is already familiar with the material from having adapted it from its playscript into a television production, is still unsatisfied with his use of the potential of the story. When he finds Columbia Pictures is willing to underwrite extensive location shooting in Bay City, Texas, the deal is on. Because Foote is a native of nearby Wharton, he acts as the company's location scout, and Mulligan is

The post-Oscar banquet finds him table-hopping and hob-nobbing with Rita Hayworth and Gina Lollobrigida.

McQueen plays an unconnected drifter whose dreams of stardom do not mesh with the real responsibility of caring for his neglected family.

Lee Remick, never better, as the essence of the Texas woman: hair drawn back from her fresh, pretty face, back straight, head high, gait strong, eyes clear and luminous, her aquiline nose and patrician forehead endowed with a woman's softness but supplemented by a jaw of granite.

delighted with the feel of the place. He is a director who believes that placing actors in a real setting enhances their credibility immeasurably, as he has proven with *Mockingbird.*

The director says of his adaptation to the screen: "We have deepened the characters and this is what opens up the movie. It was not just that we did a lot of filming outdoors in Texas. The purpose of that was to have infinite horizons. It makes the people look really finite, lost and lonely."

The film tells the tale of a ne'er-do-well, a would-be rockabilly star whose roots in his boyhood are too pervasive for him to cope with a wife and daughter concurrently. McQueen's portrayal, as guided by Mulligan, is masterfully underdone. Along the way, the picture is retitled *Highway,* and then when Glenn Yarborough records one of the Elmer Bernstein songs from the soundtrack and it hits the Top 40, the picture is renamed *Baby, the Rain Must Fall,* meaningless but a better box-office title because of the substantial radio tie-in. Yarborough does not sing in the picture; all the vocals are handled by McQueen himself, after much studio coaching and over-dubbing with technical advisor, guitarist Billy Strange.

It is a quiet little Texas pastorale, this movie, in which almost nothing happens in an action sense. McQueen gets into one knife fight, but that's all he does, physically. He plays down intensely, but Mulligan pulls the deep inner resources to the surface: "He's alive," goes Mulligan's analysis of McQueen. "He has great vitality. He's not afraid to be himself or to use himself when he acts. He has a kind of daring and theatricality, the same kind of daring as in racing his car. He does not leave that behind when he comes on stage."

McQueen plumbs the role, and the picture is often touching because of him. There are darker doings beneath the surface, through, and there are points, as in *Mockingbird,* when the picture flings itself into the Gothic with full fervor. The richness of the authentic Texas myth pervades the film.

If there is a flaw, it is that the focus is inextricably moved off the Lee Remick character and onto McQueen's. One must, after all, consider the original title: she is what the movie should be about, but it isn't. Yet, their ensemble playing convinces far more strongly than *Love With the Proper Stranger* did, though it still faces the same Hollywood para-

94

In his first movie role as a parent, McQueen is understandably discon-
certed by daughter Kimberly Block's tears.

The film's only action scenes. Compare his fighting posture with that in *Somebody Up There Likes Me*. Nine years later he is still running true to form.

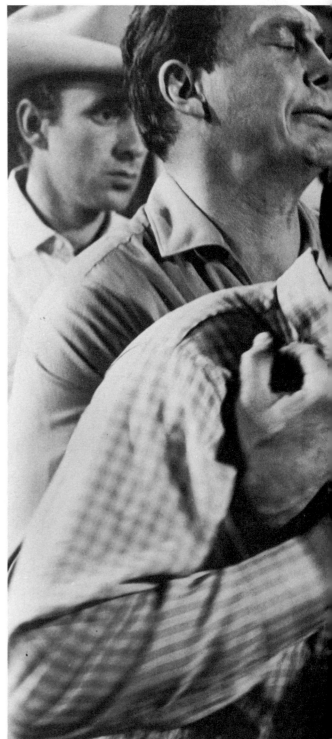

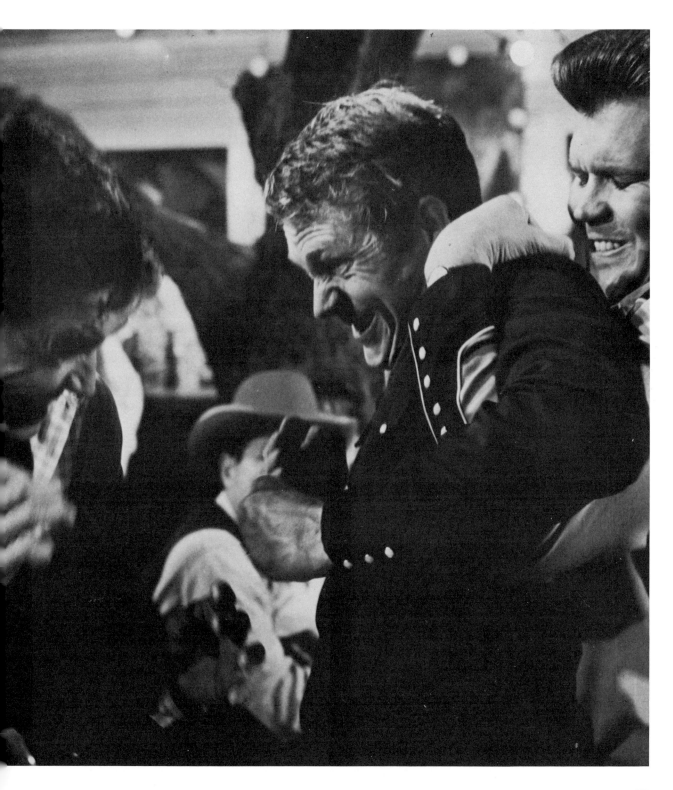

98

There's only one thing in the whole world that McQueen is afraid of in this picture, and confront it at last he must. The Gothic feel pervades, as he drives up to the old mansion, wrecking his convertible against the driveway gates. He enters, stealthily climbs the stairs, and at last stands in front of his opponent, who turns out to be a 19th century Texas grande dame, a reliquated matriarch to whom he has always been beholden.

The most unusual thing about McQueen's performance as a singer is that he does all his own singing, though there is considerable redubbing later of the title song as well as "Little Light" and "Treat Me Right."

End shot, as McQueen, a loser again, is taken away, most likely never to return.

dox of glamorous people trying to look ordinary. Somehow *Baby* escapes this danger, so deadly in *Stranger.* Perhaps McQueen's chemistry with Remick is greater than with Wood. Perhaps Horton Foote knows more about people than Arnold Schulman. Perhaps McQueen works better in a rustic milieu. Perhaps McQueen, Mulligan, and Pakula have grown to know one another better and therefore slide through the job more easily together. Perhaps it is that the simplicity of a patiently explored ballad in movie form works better than imitation urban naturalism. Or it may be all of the above.

Whatever the reasons, *Baby* remains an unsung treasure, and contains what might be the best performance Steve McQueen will ever give. And that performance leaves us with this question: had McQueen lived, would he at last won Best Actor, instead of Robert Duvall, in Foote's *Tender Mercies?* Probably so.

The Cincinnati Kid

MGM, 1965

This ad art caricature makes McQueen look more like James Coburn. (All pictures copyright © 1965 by Metro-Goldwyn-Mayer, Inc.)

CREDITS

Director, *Norman Jewison*; producer, *Martin Ransohoff*; associate producer, *John Calley*; screenplay, *Ring Lardner, Jr., Terry Southern*, from the novel by *Richard Jessup*; photographer, *Philip Lathrop* (Metrocolor); editor, *Hal Ashby*; art directors, *George W. Davis, Edward Carfagno*; music, *Lalo Schifrin*; costumes, *Donfeld*; technical advisor, *Jay Ose*.

CAST

Eric Stoner/The Cincinnati Kid *(STEVE McQUEEN)*, Lancey Howard/The Man *(Edward G. Robinson)*, Melba Nile *(Ann-Margret)*, Shooter *(Karl Malden)*, Christian Rudd *(Tuesday Weld)*, Lady Fingers *(Joan Blondell)*, William Jefferson Slade *(Rip Torn)*, Pig *(Jack Weston)*, Yeller *(Cab Calloway)*, Hoban *(Jeff Corey)*, Felix *(Theo Marcuse)*.

LOCATIONS: New Orleans.
A Filmways-Solar Picture.
Opened October 27, 1965 (102 minutes).

REVIEWS

"The film pales beside 'The Hustler,' to which it bears a striking similarity of theme and characterization" (Howard Thompson, *New York Times*).
" 'The Cincinnati Kid' is quite literally 'The Hustler' in spades. McQueen is at his 'Great Escape' best, embodying the surface cool and high intensity of the man who'll go for broke but hasn't had to" (Judith Crist, *New York Herald Tribune*).

Surprise: McQueen goes back to MGM.
Actually, he doesn't. He goes to work on a picture which MGM intends to pick up as a high-class independent production, *The Cincinnati Kid*, but it is made somewhat outside the studio's umbrella, so McQueen is satisfied. He is pleased not to be working directly for a company which he feels, albeit unfairly, hurt his career with *The Honeymoon Machine*.

101

The Smile.

Still, all runs roughly.

The source novel by Richard Jessup is purchased in February, 1964, by Martin Ransohoff, a producer who is the head of Filmways, Inc. He announces at the time that Jessup will do his own novel's adaptation for the screen, only a month after the novel has come out in hardback. The property is optioned from Little, Brown to MGM, which puts it on its roster for 1965. Ransohoff packages the deal personally, cinching it when McQueen agrees to top-line and Sam Peckinpah signs to direct.

So far, so good. But when interiors begin shooting in black-and-white in January, 1965, trouble appears as Peckinpah insists on shooting a highly verboten nude scene. Utilizing neither of the picture's femme stars Tuesday Weld or Ann-Margret, it is to be a brief glimpse of a female extra's charms, to be used only in the European release print, Peckinpah asserts.

The movie begins with a men's room fight, which McQueen settles by shoving a rusty razor blade against the interloper's jugular. The scene is included at McQueen's request because he thinks it's what his fans want to see him do.

Ransohoff is dismayed to find out, however, that Peckinpah really wants the scene included in what he calls "his" version, presumably the American cut. Ransohoff cannot make Peckinpah understand that the inclusion of even a fleeting flash of flesh will endanger the film's play-offs. And Peckinpah is incensed that a mere money man can interfere in his director's rights, even if it means worries for Ransohoff in the front office. When the fog over the pecking order has cleared, Ransohoff has fired Peckinpah, and the female extra in question disappears, too—though she will reemerge a couple of years later as Sharon Tate.

Peckinpah is replaced by 29-year-old Norman Jewison, whose flair for light comedy has been evident in amusing Doris Day trifles like *The Thrill of It All* and *Send Me No Flowers.* He does not seem qualified to shoot a big drama but for the fact that he has considerable TV experience and is used to turning things out quickly. For *The Cincinnati Kid* is already behind schedule.

Jewison is not the only substitution on the picture. Spencer Tracy had been set to play the old, established gentleman gambler in 1964, but now he bows out when he decides that he doesn't like the balance of his character against McQueen's. Edward G. Robinson takes his place, and finds himself on the same set as Joan Blondell, with whom he has not been on

McQueen gets not one girl but two, in the forms of Ann-Margret and Tuesday Weld, the latter his co-star in *Soldier in the Rain.* In scenes where the women are pictured together, such as this one, their hair colors blend like scoops in a double-dip ice cream cone.

McQueen and Ann-Margaret are named Japan's Most Popular Stars by the Japanese press this year.

103

screen since *Bullets or Ballots*, nearly 30 years ago.

The script itself passes through many changes. Originally set in St. Louis, the locale is changed to New Orleans to take advantage of the flavor of the French Quarter. With that comes the decision to shoot in Metrocolor instead of grittier black-and-white, and because of that choice the look of the picture becomes much shinier. Following writer Jessup's exit, Paddy Chayefsky comes in for a stab at the script, but whatever hand he has had in the production will be reflected neither in the tone of the picture nor in its titles. Ring Lardner, Jr., is the next fellow through the revolving door, and though he will obtain top billing on the screenplay credit, he is not the last to work on the project. With Jewison come Terry Southern and Charles Eastman to do further revisions. They incorporate McQueen's demands: he insists on a fight scene, the one that opens the picture; and he is given a chance to do his own stuntwork as he prefers, like jumping onto a locomotive moving on a roundtable in a trainyard, one of the film's few outdoor scenes. In the end, Southern is co-credited with Lardner when everybody—meaning McQueen—is satisfied at last.

Still and all, critics and public alike see *The Cincinnati Kid* for what it is, a pretty, polished ripoff of *The Hustler,* with Steve McQueen doing the Paul Newman part. It is light years away from *The Hustler*'s grimy chalk, and is, instead, handsomely shot, well-acted, and crammed with sharp editing by Hal Ashby. He will go on from here to become associate producer of the Jewison-McQueen *Thomas Crown Affair,* and thence to direct films of his own, including *Shampoo* and *Being There.* There is nothing but talent on this picture, but the subject matter is redundant and the picture frame too beautiful. Even the last ten riveting minutes, a climactic poker game between The Kid and The Man, does not salvage the film.

To McQueen's astonishment, however, he is named Best Foreign Actor for his role in *The Great Escape* by the Moscow Film Festival, and

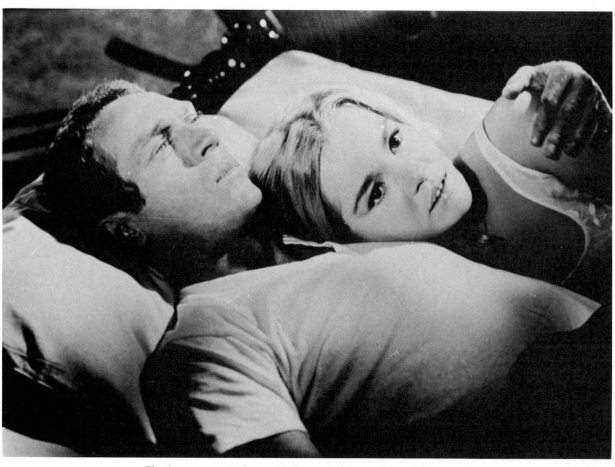

The American print leaves McQueen drifting at the end, but in Europe he winds up with Weld.

"I strongly identify with McQueen," Robinson says during the shoot. "He comes
out of the tradition of Gable, Bogie, Cagney, and even me. He's a stunner."

Strong support is offered by Malden as the expert card shark Shooter.

The Humane Society closely
investigates this brutal cock-
fight scene, but finds no
wrongdoing on the set.

That's Cab Calloway as a classy
player, with Joan Blondell
visible in the center background.

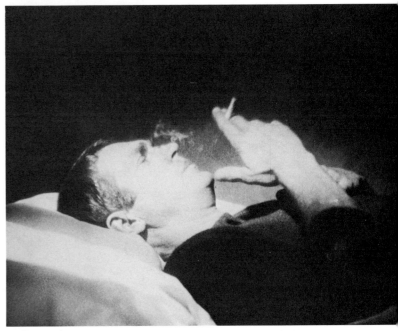

Three carefully composed character studies of McQueen as he prepares for the showpiece poker hands that conclude the movie.

a thunderstruck McQueen and family travel to the U.S.S.R. in July, 1965, to present the film officially and to act as the official American guest of honor. He has never been so far from home in his life.

Armed with this solid acting award, his first, he makes plans to attend the October premiere of *The Cincinnati Kid* in New Orleans, a benefit for the Hurricane Betsy fund, which will be the South's grandest opening since *Gone With the Wind.*

Whatever the picture's faults, no one walks out when the last game begins.

On the day of the premiere, McQueen is stunned by a long-distance call: Julia Crawford McQueen Berri, 54, proprietor of a San Francisco dress boutique purchased for her by her son, actor Steve McQueen, died today of a cerebral hemorrhage at Mt. Zion Hospital. We are very sorry, Mr. McQueen.

Shaken beyond imagining, he jets immediately to California to arrange for the funeral. He handles the death and his private sorrow with the utmost secrecy, transporting her body by private plane back to Los Angeles, where she is interred at Forest Lawn. He is close to incommunicado, breaking the silence only to request that any memorial be made in the form of donations to Boys Republic at Chino. He refuses every request for interviews: "No reporter is going to be allowed to know anything," he declares, and that is the end of the subject. Never mind that his mother was an alcoholic, that he is most likely the illegitimate product of a one-night stand, that he fantasized his parents' marriage, that he always had a love/hate thing with her, that buying her the boutique was only a way of getting close, which he never achieved. All these bitter factors, says publicist/producer/friend David Foster, are absent in the face of the funeral. "Steve might have been a bastard, literally, but he cried at the funeral. He was a lost soul." No one, not even Neile, is allowed inside.

Nevada Smith

PARAMOUNT, 1966

CREDITS

Producer-director, *Henry Hathaway;* executive producer, *Joseph E. Levine;* screenplay, *John Michael Hayes,* based on the character Nevada Smith in the novel *The Carpetbaggers,* by *Harold Robbins;* photographer, *Lucien Ballard* (EastmanColor, Panavision); editor, *Frank Bracht;* art directors, *Hal Pereira, Tambi Larsen, Al Roelofs;* music, *Alfred Newman;* costumes, *Frank Beetson, Jr.*

CAST

Nevada Smith/Max Sand *(STEVE McQUEEN),* Tom Fitch *(Karl Malden),* Jonas Cord *(Brian Keith),* Pilar *(Suzanne Pleshette),* Bill Bowdre *(Arthur Kennedy),* Neesa *(Janet Margolin),* Warden *(Howard Da Silva),* Father Zaccardi *(Raf Vallone),* Big Foot *(Pat Hingle),* Jesse Coe *(Martin Landau),* Sheriff Bonell *(Paul Fix),* Sam Sand *(Gene Evans),* Elvira McCandles *(Josephine Hutchinson),* Ben McCandles *(John Doucette),* Taka-Ta *(Iron Eyes Cody),* Saloon Girl *(Edy Williams),* Barney *(Strother Martin),* Cowboy *(L. Q. Jones).*

LOCATIONS: Lone Pine, Bishop, Mammoth, Inyo National Forest, Owens Valley, California; Independence, Louisiana.

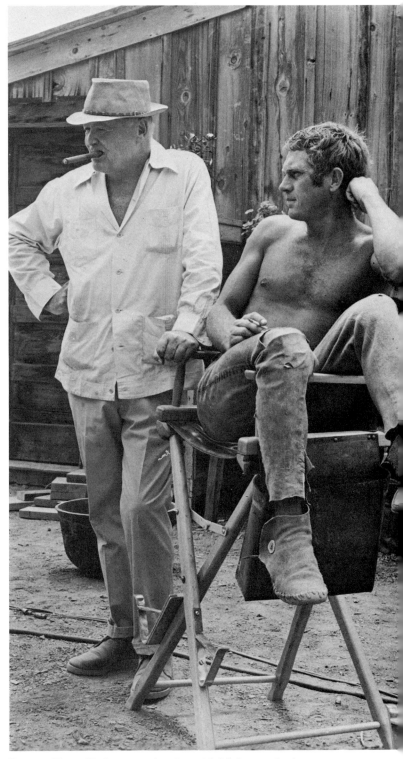

Director Henry Hathaway on location with McQueen. Just a few yards distance is the site where Hathaway had shot *Lives of a Bengal Lancer* with Gary Cooper, exactly 30 years before, also for Paramount. (All pictures copyright © 1965 by Paramount Pictures Corporation, Embassy Pictures Corporation, and Solar Productions, Inc.)

113

Two of the weapons McQueen gets to play with in the movie.

A Solar Production.
Opened June 29, 1966 (131 minutes).

REVIEWS

"The real old thing, uncut, unwatered, undiluted" (Archer Winsten, *New York Post*).
"An overstuffed Western drama. It is just too long. It is also too episodic. [But] McQueen is tight-lipped, craggy, and believable" (Vincent Canby, *New York Times*).
"You cannot connect the current Nevada with the one played by the late Alan Ladd. Everybody has missed the point which could have stimulated curiosity: how Nevada Smith got to Hollywood and into the movies. A tedious Western with too little suspense and too much talk" (Wanda Hale, *New York Daily News*).

With the booming success of *The Carpetbaggers* a year behind him, Joseph E. Levine, the last of the old-fashioned promoters, sets about looking for a suitable property with which to fill his next bank vault. In the middle of the search, he suddenly brainstorms a scheme to hatch another film from the same Harold Robbins property. The idea is originally Robbins's, whose auction of his *Carpetbaggers* best-seller nets him $300,000 Levine bucks.

114

The open shirt
invites feminine
flutters once again.

Robbins sells the book with the intent to spawn not one but three films.

The Carpetbaggers tells the story of the rise of tycoon Jonas Cord, Jr. (George Peppard), and his relationship with tempestuous thirties screen siren Rina Marlowe (Carroll Baker). Cord's father has an old friend, a kid he'd taught how to take care of himself in the Old West of the 1890's. That kid was Nevada Smith (Alan Ladd), now a cowboy movie star at the younger Cord's studio.

It is Robbins's wish that Levine follow The Carpetbaggers with Nevada's story—how he meets up with the elder Cord and becomes a man while tracking down the three cold-blooded killers who murdered his parents. That will be followed by Rina Marlowe, a tale of Hollywood glamour and tragedy.

When two Jean Harlow pictures come out in competition with each other, one of them Levine's with Carroll Baker, the Rina Marlowe project is scrapped for good, and Levine concentrates on bringing the Nevada Smith revenge epic to the screen as a big-scale Western. (The form of the film will later become known as the "prequel," a term invented in 1979 to describe Butch and Sundance: The Early Years.) Robbins ends here any intention he has had about involvement with the movie

Second-billed Karl Malden, as the central villain, is probably the only actor who can get away with saying "creepy" in a Western. His scenes with McQueen have a hammy verve to them.

as producer, now too busy to oversee things as he had on *Never Love a Stranger.*

Casting is essential, since the film is a star vehicle. Levine calls Solar and makes a deal, with the picture set as a cooperative producing venture between Levine's Embassy Pictures and McQueen's Solar, with Paramount distributing.

Logistics for the shooting schedule are staggering. Levine has hired Henry Hathaway, a highly experienced director of Westerns, including the recent *North to Alaska* and *The Sons of Katie Elder.* He will need the totality of his experience for this film, which has 68 speaking parts set amidst 42 sites. The easy interiors are completed in Hollywood in July, 1965, after McQueen returns from Moscow, and then the company is moved via 21 trucks and five buses to California's forest country. Included on the buses, as always, are the dozen members of Hathaway's stock company, whom he insists be cast in whatever film he is doing.

The rugged panoramas of California's mountain ranges provide the authentic scenery that backdrops the drama, just as the German Alps had been used in *The Great Escape.* Hathaway has come time and time again to use the Long Pine/Bishop/Mammoth area mountains in his movies, and his camera's eye never catches the same place twice, so well does he know the territory. The shame of it is that Paramount uses the wretched EastmanColor stock, which begins to fade the same year it is exposed. Most prints, even those in archives, are pale mirrors, poorly reflecting the splendid scenery audiences enjoyed in 1966.

McQueen's role, as John Michael Hayes envisions it in his script, is an aggrandized version of the bounty hunter character on *Wanted: Dead or Alive.* The difference, of course, is that Josh Randall hunted men for money on TV, whereas Nevada stalks them for blood vengeance. The hunt is the single motivation for the movie.

116

Suzanne Pleshette has a bizarre bit as a Cajun farmworker who befriends Nevada only to die of snakebite in the Louisiana swamps as he continues his quest for revenge without her.

A lobby card featuring McQueen with Brian Keith as Jonas Cord, Sr., who teaches Nevada the rudiments of survival before siring Jonas Cord, Jr., the George Peppard character in *The Carpetbaggers.*

On location: as simple a visual metaphor of McQueen's isolationist personality as one could ask for. He is simply above it all, but keeping an eye on everything.

117

As a half-Kiowa, McQueen brings to his part his own lithe catlike grace, endowing his movements with Indian body language. His performance demands that the audience accept this 36-year-old California blond as a part-Indian teenager, at least in the film's opening quarter. Yet McQueen completely gets away with his improbable impersonation because he is in such terrific shape. He really can look half his age, the rashness of youth radiating from his bronzed, flushed skin.

What McQueen brings to the movie, though, is not reciprocated. He finds himself in a long-winded, short-actioned, episodic, cliché-ridden Western that at times seems tedious, if not endless. The film follows Nevada every step of the way as he relentlessly tracks down and executes each of his parents' killers (Karl Malden, Martin Landau, and Arthur Kennedy). There is an overt emphasis on religion, but that must be an attempt to offset criticism of the film's real joy of violence. Audiences are always delighted when Nevada at last is twisting a knife into Landau's guts, for instance. And even these questionably exciting moments are few and far between in this two-hours-plus horse opera.

At 131 minutes, the film is still shorter than it could have been. Editors labor furiously trying to bring its running time down. They chop anything. Joanna Moore's role as Landau's grateful widow is cut down to so little that her name isn't even listed in the credits any more. In the end, though, there is just so much they can eliminate.

Yet the picture is a smash—overseas. It is an official invited entry in the San Sebastian Film Festival. In Trinidad, mounted police are called four times in one day to quiet frenzied crowds who are breaking down the theater's doors to get in to see the movie. Somebody out there likes the movie: it can only be because McQueen is garnering huge fans in England, Europe, and Japan, audiences who see him as some kind of quintessential American.

McQueen himself is noncommittal about *Nevada Smith*. He likes it, all right, and finds its bloodthirstiness moral in the light of what has caused it. He'd've done the same thing, he shrugs. The picture is over. He has his mind on other things, including another Levine project.

Then Robert Wise reenters McQueen's life with something better, an offer that will take Steve heartbreakingly close to the Oscar he has coveted since 1958. It is an offer he cannot refuse.

Off-set, yakking with Kennedy.

Character portrait of Nevada Smith, the former Max Sand.

The Sand Pebbles

20TH CENTURY-FOX, 1966

CREDITS

Producer-director, *Robert Wise;* associate producer, second unit director, *Charles Maguire;* screenplay, *Richard Anderson,* from the novel by *Richard McKenna;* photographer, *Joseph MacDonald* (DeLuxe Color, Panavision); editor, *William Reynolds;* production design, *Boris Leven;* music, *Jerry Goldsmith;* costumes, *Renie;* technical advisor, *Harvey Misiner,* MMC, USN (Ret.); diversions, *Irving Schwartz.**

CAST

Jake Holman *(STEVE McQUEEN),* Frenchy *(Richard Attenborough),* Captain *(Richard Crenna),* Shirley Eckert *(Candice Bergen),* Maily *(Marayat Andriane),* Po-Han *(Mako),* Mr. Jameson *(Larry Gates),* Ensign Bordelles *(Charles Robinson),* Stawski *(Simon Oakland),* Crosley *(Gavin McLeod),* Shanahan *(Joseph di Reda).*

*A credit producer-director Wise gave in thanks to the combined efforts of actors Gavin McLeod and Joe di Reda, who cheered the crew during inclement weather and civil disturbances on location.

LOCATIONS: Taiwan, Hong Kong.
An Argyle-Solar Picture.
Opened: December 20, 1966 (193 minutes).

REVIEWS

"Performed by Steve McQueen with the most restrained, honest, heartfelt acting he has ever done" (Bosley Crowther, *New York Times*).
"Over three hours of tedium, interspersed with a blood-spattered schmaltz-spangled compendium of screenplay clichés" (Judith Crist, *World Journal Tribune*).
"Fails, finally, to transcend itself as a melodrama used as star-vehicle" (Archer Winsten, *New York Post*).

Bad movie or not, *Nevada Smith* makes a lot of money, and Levine wants McQueen again to star in his pet project, *The Ski Bum,* from the Romain Gary novel. The option has remained in Levine's files for some time because he hasn't found the right man for the job. He needs an athlete with a ton of sex appeal and a long ton of box-office ability. Because of his

Hard and tough in his only Oscar-nominated performance. (All pictures copyright © 1967 by 20th Century-Fox Film Corporation)

Off-duty McQueen chats up a hostess of the Red Candle Happiness Inn.

success within the Levine organization, McQueen finds he is being courted for the role for a 1967 release.

He's looking seriously at it when Robert Wise comes along with a deal for $250,000 plus a star's percentage to headline his epic tale of China adventure, *The Sand Pebbles*. It is by far the most lucrative salary and prestigious part he has ever received, and he accepts on both counts.

Robert Anderson's screenplay, as thick as a telephone book, is adapted from a mammoth best-selling novel by Richard McKenna, who

has based his story on his experiences as an enlisted Navy man stationed in China for 22 years. Its setting of 1926 China on the Yangtze River has no overt political relevance to the Vietnam War current and in full flame, but there is nevertheless strong implication of allegory. Once a simple sailor, McKenna sees his novel hit the top of sales lists, become a Book-of-the-Month Club selection, go into serialization in the *Saturday Evening Post*, and earn him the $10,000 Harper Prize for a first novel. In September, 1962, he receives an undisclosed rights purchase price estimated to

121

be $300,000 for the movie rights. Sadly, McKenna dies before the story hits the cameras.

The projected film, to be produced and directed by Wise, had once been set as a Mirisch production for United Artists, but a dispute over budget and contractual terms had turned the picture around to 20th Century-Fox instead. Wise had then begun pre-production rolling, only to find its pre-production one-rouse. In early 1963, McQueen's name was mentioned for the first time, but it was rejected for not yet being a big enough name.

Meanwhile, Wise had talked Fox into giving him *The Sound of Music* to do while the hurdles on *The Sand Pebbles* were being steadily overcome, one by one. William Wyler, who had been set to direct the musical, had a falling-out with the studio, and Wise was able to take over the project. It took a year-and-a-half of his life to make, but its now legendary earnings come as such a surprise to Fox that they give Wise carte blanche to create *The Sand Pebbles*.

In that 18-month interim, however, Steve McQueen has become a full-fledged star. Wise is all for casting him, thinks him perfect for the role, better even than Paul Newman, who has read the script and turned it down. Wise himself goes to McQueen's hilltop estate, and marvels that the actor, in a single decade, "has gone from being broke and hungry to living in a mansion on a hill." McQueen is signed, but only after a contract proviso allowing his whole family to accompany him to the Far East.

Fox has optimistically set three big road-shows for its 1966 fiscal year: *The Blue Max*, *The Bible*, and *The Sand Pebbles*, which is its fondest hope, a big-budgeted $6 million war drama. So massive has *The Sound of Music*'s success turned out to be that Fox confidently proclaims that its upcoming *Sand Pebbles* will follow the musical's run at New York's Rivoli Theater as the Christmas, 1966, attraction. The booking is made the previous May.

No expense is spared in shooting the picture using authentic Oriental locations, the realness of locale being a prime Wise dictate.

Principal photography commences in November, 1965, with Wise and a crew of 100 embarking for the set-ups scheduled in Taiwan, the first American film made there with the complete approval of the Chiang Kai-shek

Alexandra Hay is briefly considered for the girl's part, but Candice Bergen's sincerity in wanting to be taken seriously leads to her being cast instead.

Oriental actor Mako doesn't know yet what his grisly end in the film will be: death by skinning while still alive.

regime. Six weeks in Hong Kong follow as Wise shoots the biggest set-piece of the film, a water battle between the *San Pablo* (thus the title) and 30 Chinese junks. Two months of interiors in Hollywood complete production. And when that is done, the picture's budget has doubled.

"It's the most difficult picture I ever made," recalls Wise a generation later, and truly the problems of making *The Sand Pebbles* would have defeated almost anyone else. Assembling the pieces is ambitious: seven antique autos imported from Australia, 50 refurbished rickshaws, daily calls for 300 to 1500 extras clothed in thousands of costumes, all with little benefit of the English language.

Then there's the weather. The lousiest: 86 degrees one day, 30 the next. Rain, rain, rain, rain, rain, rain, rain. The weather causes riots among the bored natives. Wise turns to shooting interiors, waiting for the exteriors to clear, and has the entire set that is the *San Pablo* crew's living quarters dismantled in Hollywood and shipped to Taipei. He's too efficient for his

Anti-American demonstrations drive home the Vietnam allegory.

124

Grim, quiet determination mark McQueen's acting. It is clear why the Academy singled him out.

own good, though, and with interiors quickly finished, everyone just sits around waiting for the rain and the riots to end.

Meanwhile, the boat sits in the water, a flat-bottomed prop that cannot move under its own power. At $250,000 it is the most expensive prop ever built for a movie (and would have cost at least a million if constructed in the U.S., Wise estimates). It is based on the USS *Villa Lobos*, a Spanish ship seized during the Spanish-American War and drafted for service in the Far East, where it sank in the Philippines in 1929. Working from blueprints of the *Villa Lobos*, the movie's *San Pablo* is an authentic recreation, with modifications, of American gunboat design of the early 20th century. Just in case, the costly full-sized prop is insured against everything up to and including submarine attack.

Adapting a fighting ship for a film company's convenience consists of drilling small holes around the decks for catwalks which are utilized for tracking shots. The boat is photographed from afar using 20-foot-high camera platforms planted in the mud of Taiwan's Keelung and Tam Sui rivers. Press reports after the film claim the boat becomes a floating dormitory for American construction crews working behind Vietnamese battle lines. Other sources indicate that it is more a waterborne whorehouse than a sleeping quarters. Probably both.

Everything mounts up: delays, slow construction, bad weather. McQueen and Wise differ often on how a scene should be shot, and Wise acquiesces by shooting two versions of the scenes in question. Wise's editorial sense prevails and none of McQueen's versions end up in the final print. At least, however, there is a final print, which many Jeremiahs along the way have predicted there would not be.

The picture opens on schedule, with McQueen uncharacteristically spending ten days in New York promoting the movie. When

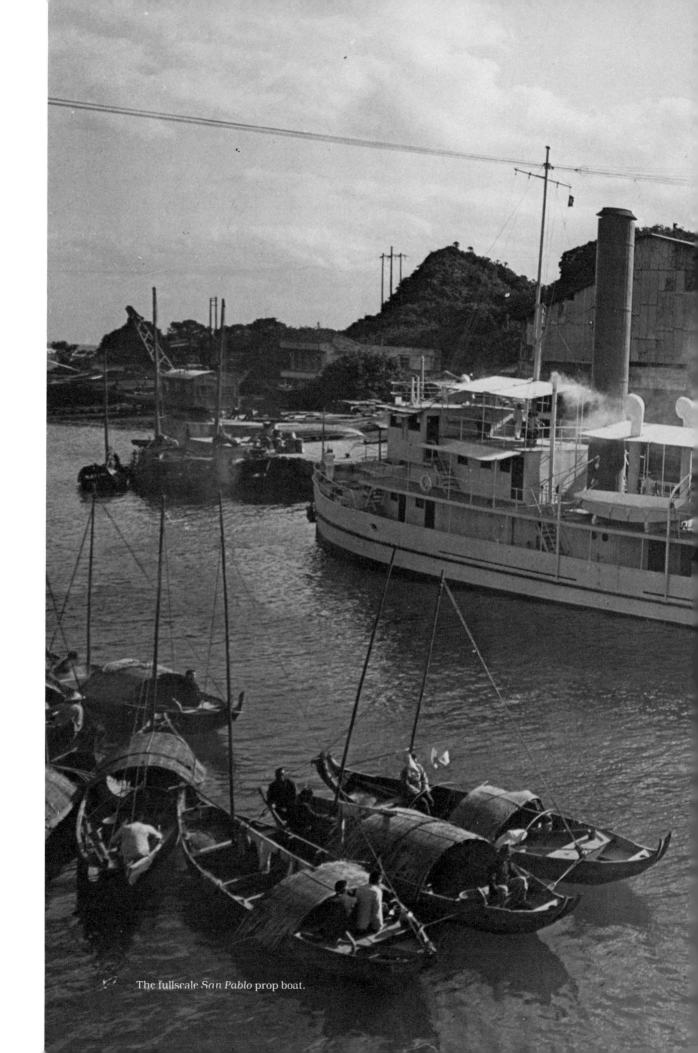
The fullscale *San Pablo* prop boat.

the Oscar nominations come out a couple of months later, it is allotted eight nominations. But the Best Picture and cinematography awards go to *A Man for All Seasons;* Mako loses Best Supporting Actor to Walter Matthau in *The Fortune Cookie;* art and set decoration miss out to *Fantastic Voyage;* sound and editing both go to *Grand Prix;* and the music score bows to *Born Free.*

Best Actor: the nominees are Alan Arkin for *The Russians Are Coming,* Michael Caine for *Alfie,* Richard Burton for *Who's Afraid of Virginia Woolf,* Paul Scofield for *A Man for All Seasons,* and Steve McQueen for *The Sand Pebbles.* And the winner is: Paul Scofield.

"So real, so right," Wise has praised McQueen's performance. But the Academy has had another one of its British years and, boy howdy, Steve McQueen is anything but British.

He is unhappy. He has spent many months on Taiwan with his family, living in one room in the middle of a rice paddy. Neile has turned down an offer to star with Brando in something called *Southwest to Sonora* to go with her man halfway around the world. "I don't think a married man should ever be left alone for more than two weeks," she explains. His winning World Film Favorite, along with Julie Andrews, at the Golden Globes is some consolation, but not enough to make up for what he

McQueen in action against a Chinese bit player.

End of the movie: McQueen sits waiting to die but intent on taking a few with him. McQueen says he himself would have run, not stayed.

has had to endure abroad. "Anything I ever did wrong, I paid for in Taiwan," he ruefully proclaims.

And while he feels it is the best picture he has ever made, McQueen hates himself in the Jake Holman role. Part of it comes from having lived through the grueling shoot. Part of it is due to his feeling that the character didn't act as McQueen himself would have. He is at odds with his reel life and his real life.

Failing to understand completely his dissatisfaction, he takes the family to Alaska on a fishing vacation. It isn't enough, so he leaves the movie industry for one full year.

At the premiere: (l to r), Robert Wise, Patricia Wise, Neile Adams McQueen, McQueen.

130

The Thomas Crown Affair

UNITED ARTISTS, 1968

CREDITS

Producer-director, *Norman Jewison;* associate producer, *Hal Ashby;* screenplay *Alan R. Trustman;* photographer, *Haskell Wexler* (DeLuxe Color); editor, *Hal Ashby;* multiple screens and titles, *Pablo Ferro Films;* art director, *Robert Boyle;* music, *Michel Legrand;* Faye Dunaway's costumes, *Theadora Van Runkle;* Steve McQueen's costumes, *Ron Postal;* technical advisors, *Alfred Sheinwald, Gary Wooten;* casting, *Lynn Stalmaster.*

CAST

Thomas Crown *(STEVE McQUEEN)*, Vicky Anderson *(Faye Dunaway)*, Eddy Malone *(Paul Burke)*, Erwin Weaver *(Jack Weston)*, Carol *(Yaphet Kotto)*, Sandy *(Biff McGuire)*, Gwen *(Astrid Heeren)*, sketch artist *(Nikita Knatz)*.

LOCATIONS: Boston.
A Mirisch-Simkoe-Solar Production.
SHOOTING TITLES: *The Crown Caper, Thomas Crown, Esq., Thomas Crown and Company.*
MPAA rating: Suggested for Mature Audiences.
Opened June 26, 1968 (102 minutes).

McQueen with director Jewison, the hottest director in Hollywood since he has just accumulated five Oscars, including Best Picture, for *In the Heat of the Night.* (All pictures copyright © 1968 by United Artists)

131

One of the attractive studio interiors, built in Los Angeles for seven weeks
of work, following Boston location-shooting.

The Smile: the man has just stolen $2½ million from his own bank.

REVIEWS

"There is a long, soon-to-be-famous kissing scene that is so misdirected one thinks of Edsels on a summer's night. McQueen is always special, and although his role is too indoors and formal, he does get a chance to race across the desert or fly a glider or lie on a beach, in the casual-intense work he is best at" (Renata Adler, *New York Times*).

"McQueen, dashing around with verve, unlimited energy and bright, inquiring eyes, makes you wonder if he knows he's hatching something almost akin to a turkey" (Archer Winsten, *New York Post*).

"A polished McQueen, minus his motorcyclist's mumble, shows a whole new facet of his active personality. He is cast most successfully" (Kathleen Carroll, *New York Daily News*).

He is true to his word, making no films for a full year.

Well, he kind of makes one: "The Coming of the Roads" for KABC-TV in Los Angeles. Broadcast on September 17, 1966, it is a 30-minute documentary about the ruination of the Santa Monica Mountains. It is a plea for conservation but also for privacy, since it's his neighborhood, and squabbles with other local landowners make the local newspapers' front pages.

He has also read over 200 scripts looking for the right vehicle, and he's tired of hunting for something that doesn't have him behind a steering wheel with a gun in his hand. Bored, he talks about opening a restaurant on the Sunset Strip to serve nothing but Mexican food, his favorite. His partner will be longtime buddy Elmer Valentine, who owns the Whisky a Go Go. The name of the restaurant? "La Rebellion de Los Adolescentes."

This little food fantasy is no substitute, however, for going back into pictures, and so late 1966 brings McQueen to Warner Brothers to sign an agreement partnering the studio with his Solar Productions. "I ran out of money so I had to go back to work," he explains.

The deal is for him to produce six pictures for the studio, starring himself in three, though he is to be uncredited as the producer. Terms are set at $750,000 per film plus a whopping 50 percent of the profits, the press reports. His 61 percent interest in Solar also nets him a sizable six-figure annual income, making him one of the highest paid stars in the world.

More industry acclaim comes his way the following March, when he places his signature and footprints into the 153rd cement block at Grauman's Chinese Theater in Hollywood. He roars up in his burgundy Ferrari to the delight of 2000 kids who are on Easter vacation. The event is televised live by KTLA. And though he has been seen in nothing for a year, he still places tenth in *Boxoffice* magazine's annual popularity poll. The year before, with an Oscar nomination to his credit, he hadn't even placed.

Now there has been some talk about the possibility of his traveling back to Russia to shoot *The Kremlin Letter* for John Huston in Moscow. But his experiences with Norman Jewison on *The Cincinnati Kid*, especially his stylish use of camerawork, leads McQueen to contact the by-now Oscar-winning director to helm the new film tentatively titled *The Crown Caper*. The film will go through several title changes before settling on the mildly double-entendre *Thomas Crown Affair*.

The story comes from Boston attorney Alan Trustman, who shows the tight 59-page script to Jewison, who options it as his next project. Jewison has just been to Montreal for the Expo '67 exhibition, and has been particularly impressed by the short experimental film *A Place to Stand*. Intrigued by the as yet unexplored commercial potential of the multiple screen technique, Jewison splices the process into the *Crown* project.

That decision, plus the casting of McQueen, make the movie bankable. Then Jewison tops himself, endowing the film with a satiny patina of chic, personified by Faye Dunaway. Starting

A lobby card advertises one of the film's big scenes, the polo match where McQueen and Dunaway meet.

The polo game is a fusion of dozens of images capturing many angles of the event at once. Pablo Ferro Films is visual designer.

with a splash in *Bonnie and Clyde,* she has made five pictures in the last year, graduating from super-starlet to leading lady. She loves getting to work with McQueen: "He stimulates that cuddly feeling. He's the misunderstood bad guy you're sure you can cure with a little warmth and some home cooking." She is not talking about Thomas Crown.

She also loves being given some 30 costumes to wear as she clothes-horses her way through this tale of a man who robs his own banks and the exceedingly well-dressed insurance investigator who always gets her man.

Initial advertising emphasizes the caper aspect: "Introducing an exciting new company that brings a much-needed lift to the field of crime." But first reviews cling to another factor, and the ads quickly change to emphasize The Kiss.

Despite the robberies and the elegant accoutrements and the polo game and the glider sequence and all those cute little multiple screens, The Kiss is the real set-piece of *The Thomas Crown Affair.* It springs from The Chess Game, a five-minute sequence comparable to the famed dinner scene from *Tom Jones.*

Instead of being gleefully ribald like Tony Richardson, though, Jewison goes for the somberly erotic. For the first time in the history of the American cinema, tonguey kisses are freely visible between two Big Stars. Penelope Gilliatt says the close-ups remind her of "two goldfish going after the same crumb." Audiences, however, think it's great and that's why they go to see it, sold by word-of-mouth.

McQueen earns his $700,000 salary by doing once again what comes naturally. While posing as a suave, well-educated and well-heeled banker might seem blatant miscasting, he is still McQueen, recognizably and uniquely. Since the film is made under the Solar umbrella, he exercises his usual script control, inserting plenty of visual reminders that this is a McQueen picture. A lot is already in the script, like a sky-diving sequence he simply changes to a glider scene. He does his own polo stunting on location at the Hamilton, Massachusetts, Myopia Hunt Club, trying hard to maintain the rigid correctness of the English saddle against his body's kinesthetic memory-sense of riding in the armchair-like Western saddle.

It has been many years since anyone has made a Gee-I-wonder-what-she's-going-to-wear-next picture. An appreciative McQueen retains costume designer Theadora Van Runkle for future projects.

The Kiss: until those lips touch, there is nothing more overt than Dunaway stroking a rook or nibbling the end of a digit. The scene leads to the picture's being tagged "Suggested for Mature Audiences."

And now that he heads the production he willingly tub-thumps. Familiar with Boston bluebloods from six weeks of location shooting, he returns June 9, 1968, to headline a $100-per-ticket black-tie premiere benefit for the Brookwood School and the New England Aquarium. Then he's off for a 36-city promotional tour. How unlike Steve, think his friends from the old days.

The music by Michel Legrand also helps sell the picture, and his song, "The Windmills of Your Mind," wins an Oscar the following April, 1969. The score is also nominated but loses to

137

The most bizarre thing about the chess sequence, however, is the attendant publicity sheet that sober-facedly asserts that the moves in the game are from a classic match played in 1899 in Vienna by Masters Zeissl and Walthoffen. Honest.

John Barry's compositions for *The Lion in Winter.*

When the returns are in, the $4 million *Thomas Crown Affair* has, as expected, carried off a bundle. Part of the hefty receipts have been known long in advance, since the film is presented as a rare blind-bid product to exhibi-tors, who gladly fork over guaranteed advances, knowing that a McQueen picture will fill the theaters. They are proven correct.

Curiously, the film becomes and remains a favorite of Jimmy Carter, who as President will screen the picture over and over in the White House. Make of that what you will.

138

The $350 three-piece suit is by Beverly Hills tailor Ron Postal. The watch is
a $2250 Patek Philippe. The Phi Beta Kappa key is borrowed from one of
the set designers.

Despite the fact that he hates heights, McQueen does much of his own gliding in this sequence.

McQueen features two scenes with dune buggies, his latest speed obsession in real life. The one he drives in the movie is a modification of this unit, designed for him by friend Pete Condos and manufactured by McQueen subsidiary Solar Plastics and Engineering. The company goes out of business due to operating losses, but McQueen holds onto the buggies.

Original lobby card for *Bullitt*. (All pictures copyright
© 1968 by Warner Bros.-7 Arts, Inc.)

Bullitt

WARNER BROTHERS, 1968

CREDITS

Director, *Peter Yates;* producer, *Philip D'Antoni;* executive producer, *Robert Relyea;* screenplay, *Alan R. Trustman, Harry Kleiner,* from the novel *Mute Witness,* by *Robert L. Pike;* photographer, *William A. Fraker* (Technicolor); editor, *Frank O. Keller;* art director, *Albert Brenner;* music, *Lalo Schifrin;* costumes, *Alan Levine, Theadora Van Runkle;* titles, *Pablo Ferro Films.*

CAST

Lt. Frank Bullitt *(STEVE McQUEEN),* Walter Chalmers *(Robert Vaughn),* Cathy *(Jacqueline Bisset),* Delgetti *(Don Gordon),* Weissberg/Cab driver *(Robert Duvall),* Capt. Sam Bennet *(Simon Oakland),* Capt. Baker *(Norman Fell),* Carl Stanton *(Carl Reindel),* Albert Edward Renick *(Felice Orlandi),* Pete Ross *(Vic Tayback).*

LOCATIONS: San Francisco.
A Solar Production.
Opened October 17, 1968 (114 minutes).

Real locations authenticize the picture in a
way no Burbank backlot ever could.

141

REVIEWS

"A terrific movie, just right for Steve McQueen—fast, well-acted, written the way people talk. McQueen simply gets better all the time" (Renata Adler, *New York Times*).

"McQueen keeps his cool as only he can, now that Bogart's long gone. The best, most exciting car chase the movies have ever put on film. McQueen, motorcycle and auto racer, knew what he was doing and what had to be done" (Archer Winsten, *New York Post*).

"McQueen joins the ranks of top movie detectives. His portrayal is cool, calm, casual, and convincing" (Ann Guarino, *New York Daily News*).

"A curiously exhilarating mixture of reality and fantasy, so actual that at times one could almost swear that the fictional adventures must have been shot with concealed cameras" (Tom Milne, *The Sunday Observer*).

During the on-location Boston shooting of *Crown*, McQueen has met with real local bankers, who are interested in his project for some as-yet formless $5 million Western. But they want to see how his upcoming *Bullitt* is going to do first.

They have two reasons for their hesitation. First, even after four smashes in a row, McQueen has not been on top for all that long. They want to make sure he's a lasting audience draw before investing in him. Second, *Bullitt* is a very personal property for Steve, something that for the first time he himself has gone out and bought as his own vehicle, using Solar. An auteur piece. How good would their boy's eye be in choosing his own starring properties?

Cameraman Bill Fraker adopts a low-angle, highly exaggerated style that approximates the extreme look of the comic strip.

142

McQueen with movie girlfriend Jacqueline Bisset, who tells Rona Barrett it is difficult
to work with him: "It was confusing to me because he spoke in American slang, and I
could hardly understand him. He's a nervous man when he's working. He'd repeatedly
come over to me and say, 'We've got to discuss this scene,' and then someone would call
him away and we'd never get around to it."

Duvall, still a nobody, makes an impression in his small taxidriver role.

Now, if *Bullitt* turns out to be no more than an overgrown home movie, they'll forget it. But if he shows a shrewdness beyond his own presentation as a star, that will be something else.

It is definitely something else. *Bullitt* is the film that cements Steve McQueen as the greatest American action/adventure star: the rebel who is a hero of the Old West *(The Magnificent Seven)*, of World War II *(The Great Escape)*, and now of the side of law and order. It will become his own favorite film, and it is the one for which he is best remembered.

Here's how *Bullitt* comes about. Phil D'Antoni, a former TV producer, has optioned the source novel *Mute Witness*, by Robert L. Pike (a pseudonym for author Robert L. Fish). He wants Spencer Tracy for it, to play the book's luckless cop Clancy from New York's 52nd Precinct. With McQueen's involvement now piqueing Warner Brothers' interest, D'Antoni orders a rewrite, turning it into a police flick set in San Francisco and featuring a detective hero considerably younger than Tracy. He takes

it to Solar, Solar takes it to Warners, and Warners finances the picture, though it will be made entirely by Solar.

The only thing worrying Warners is the fact that McQueen insists on shooting the picture on location. He is at particular loggerheads with WB executive vice-president in charge of production Kenneth Hyman, who wants the movie shot on the back lot. "You want it like that, you can shove the goddamn picture," McQueen retorts, and the film moves to San Francisco. (Hyman tries later to corral McQueen's bike-riding off the set, and finds his memo returned with placement instructions, corners and all.)

Warners is worried that the film will turn out to be a domestic runaway, only 400 miles from home but out of their control. They still approve the package, though, appropriating a whopping $5 million for the production ($1 million alone going to McQueen). It is the first film ever shot on location with an all-Hollywood crew, the first major movie to break free of

144

(Opposite page) McQueen plays Frank Bullitt with firm humorlessness, giving one of the surest, evenest performances of his career, reacting, never acting out, virtually directing himself, designing with Yates and Fraker the form and direction of the character.

Inches from the set, McQueen confers with Robert Vaughn, who plays the cold and oily politico opposing Lt. Bullitt. Acquainted from their work together in *The Magnificent Seven*, they will appear again in *The Towering Inferno*.

studio dependence, and, incidentally, the first picture to use the new, lightweight Arriflex cameras exclusively.

The script is polished by Alan Trustman, the lawyer who wrote *Thomas Crown*, and co-written by Harry Kleiner, who will soon contribute a racing script about Le Mans. The director is Britisher Peter Yates, signed because he has just directed a dynamite chase scene in *Robbery*, and because the British are already invading the town (John Schlesinger is doing *Midnight Cowboy*, Richard Lester has just finished *Petulia*). Yates throws himself quite boldly into the picture, even shooting some of the big chase sequence himself using a hand-held camera.

The chase is the thing. McQueen wants everyone to remember it. According to Yates, McQueen does all his own driving for the 12-minute sequence. Other sources indicate McQueen awakes one morning to find most of his driving has already been done for him, particularly the hill-jumping shots. Some rumors attribute only a third of the actual maneuvering to McQueen, with Bud Ekins (who also stunt-skids a bike in front of a car) doing the jumps and Carey Loftin driving

146

through the fiery gas-station explosion, just to make sure nothing happens to the star. Even going through the film frame by frame doesn't reveal anything because it all goes by so fast in such a blur of movement.

It is, after all, very difficult to keep up with cars going 110 mph. What we have here is a souped-up 390 GT Mustang, McQueen's wheels, chasing a 440 Magnum Dodge full of the bad guys (themselves pursued by a hot Chevy camera car dubbed the Bullittmobile).

This scene alone takes up two weeks, a sixth of the shooting schedule. Daily shooting starts

Detective Lieutenant Frank Bullitt is assigned by Captain Bennet (Simon Oakland) to guard a hoodlum-on-the-lam who is to be a witness at a coming Senate crime hearing. Looking on are Captain Baker (Norman Fell) and Detective Delgetti (Don Gordon), the latter assigned to work with Bullitt.

Bullitt and Delgetti rush to the hospital, where a young Black surgeon (Georg S. Brown) tries in vain to save the hoodlum's life. Bullitt is convinced the killing was a set-up, and arranges to have the body removed from the hospital, as though the hoodlum were still alive, so that the detectives may have time to hunt the killers.

at 7:30 A.M., and goes on until dark; each move is rehearsed slowly until the stunt is brought up to speed. Loftin runs the rehearsals. The Charger is handled by Bill Hickman, a McQueen confederate and bike champ who will go on from here to stage the movies' next great chase scene in *The French Connection*, also produced by D'Antoni. Fraker coordinates everything with a battery-run camera inside the Mustang for POV, two fixed-position cameras on the street, and a platform camera mounted on the Bullittmobile. Then the whole thing is assembled by editor Frank Keller, who wins an Oscar the next year for his troubles (the film does, however, loses its other nomination, for Best Sound, to *Oliver!*).

McQueen regards the chase as a cogent demonstration of his driving prowess for his public. A chance for him to play on a giant roadrace set. He is entranced by the undeniable realness of the chase: no relying on a fake insert shot of the speedometer to let you know how fast it's supposed to be going. You're right in the car, so you know how fast without looking. The point-of-view shot is something he picks up later for *Le Mans*. Yates and Fraker teach him how here and now.

There is another side to the movie, however, and it's called the plot. The movie feels and looks like one of the toughest, hardest, most stylish detective pictures ever made, so definite and alone in its tone and mood that Robert Altman will parody it almost verbatim a few years later in his *Brewster McCloud*. Yet the storyline is nearly incomprehensible. It appears to be something about Frank Bullitt (the man's name is his autobiography) having to protect a key witness from Mafia bullets. But the guy gets killed, so Bullitt has to pretend he isn't dead so that the killers . . . oh, well, you're really not there for the story, right? You want to see the man drive. Then watch. As Warren Weith points out, Bullitt and his Mustang are the same thing: "[The car is] hubcapless, with a dull black paint job that looked like it had been applied with a whisk broom. It was, in fact, the automotive counterpart of the hero. No glitter, but all guts."

Even with its impenetrable storyline, *Bullitt* makes a mint: $19 million in America alone, a major major hit. "You take something out, you have to put something back," McQueen has always said. While on location, he had hired

148

McQueen does, of course, get to shoot people. The fans demand.

A dangerous scene in which McQueen chases the bad guy all over the runways at San Francisco International Airport. He does everything himself. Of course.

McQueen grabs an apple and a cigarette between takes. The apple will not keep the doctor away.

300 underprivileged kids from San Francisco's depressed Hunter's Point district to act as extras. Now he donates a swimming pool to their neighborhood recreation park. (He also supports the Youth Studies Center at USC and the Kidney Foundation; once a year he drives a truckload of food, clothing, and medical supplies to the poverty-ridden Indians of the Four Corners area where New Mexico, Colorado, Utah, and Arizona touch borders; he has been honored for his charitable work by the United Jewish Welfare Fund; and he continues his scholarships and personal appearance at his Chino alma mater).

And so the boys in Boston are more than willing to talk about financing that $5 million Western.

This is it. McQueen is hotter than he has ever been. He's earning a million per picture now, and Boston has simply got to have him before anyone else gets him. They give him the go-ahead, but the Western never materializes.

For he has other things on his mind. There is *Yucatan*, for instance, about a professional adventurer who rides his bike through the Mexican wilderness to find ancient wells where Mayan maidens were sacrificed a thousand years ago. The prize: the fabulous jewels with

With presenter Leslie Caron at the 1969 Golden Globes. The Hollywood Foreign Press Association has just awarded him the title "World Film Favorite." Streisand gets the distaff equivalent.

which the high priests bedecked their victims. It is McQueen's idea from the beginning, and he gives his story idea to his new writer friend Harry Kleiner. Steve scouts five hundred miles' worth of Mexican locations while Kleiner turns the story into a script. But the budget escalates from $3 million to $7 million and financing is difficult. Then McQueen finds out he can't do any of the skin-diving himself because he has developed an inner ear problem that precludes scuba. If he can't do the stunts himself, he won't do the picture. So the picture is left in the typewriter.

Then there is *Man on a Nylon String*, a Warners-Solar collaboration which will be a murder mystery set in the Swiss Alps, from the novel by Whit Masterson and a script by Edward Anhalt. It is scheduled to start principal photography in fall 1967, under George Roy Hill's direction. The mountaineering adventure is budgeted at a fairly low $1.4 million, but when McQueen angrily leaves Warners (it's about to happen) the project goes ironically to director Mark Rydell, who introduced Neile to Steve back in 1966. There the word "nylon" is

Neile remains in Los Angeles with the children until she hears Steve is risking his life behind the wheel again. She catches the next flight to San Francisco.

151

excised from its title, but eventually it is canceled. It's okay by McQueen—his acrophobia was giving him trepidation about the film anyway.

Swap, from the spy novel *The Cold War Swap* by Ross Thomas. It is announced in January, 1967, by its producer Hillard Elkins (also McQueen's personal manager) as a late 1967 release. Thomas, winner of the 1966 Edgar Allan Poe award from the Mystery Writers of America, has sold his book for $50,000, and is pleased both with the intended star and that it will be released by Paramount. McQueen suggests John Sturges as director, and, concerned as they both always are about authentic locations, plans are drawn to attempt shooting at least part of the picture in East Berlin. But McQueen is also involved in designing his own car for the first time, the "Baja Bucket," which he is anxious to test in Nevada's gruelling Stardust 7-11 marathon. The film is never made.

He thinks about doing *Applegate's Gold*, from a Western novel by Parker Bonner (pseudonym for Todhunter Ballard). As soon as the Solar board of directors starts talking about a title change, to avoid comparisons with the wretched *McKenna's Gold*, currently on the nation's screens, McQueen loses interest.

He talks about *Suddenly Single*, a Southern California-based comedy. Oh, yes, he remembers, he hates himself in comedy. Doesn't do it. He discusses doing one picture outside Solar's aegis, *The Yards at Essendorf*, another war film to be directed by John Sturges, whom McQueen regards as "the greatest action director." Nothing comes of it. He considers a $10 million partnership with Montgomery Ward's to develop the "McQueen Motorcycle," but it is shelved. He thinks it's just as well; bike companies have been after him since *The Great Escape* to endorse their machines, and he has always refused (although in 1973 he will finally break down and accept a million dollars to shoot a Honda commercial that will be seen only in Japan, where he is something beyond a superstar; the ad features him riding and emphasizing safety first). Another family plan that bites the dust is the invitation to Neile to play Tiger Lily in a new movie musical of *Peter Pan*. McQueen's woman does not work. Period.

Meanwhile, the rewards of *Bullitt* are pouring in. It has emerged by far the biggest money-maker of his 18-picture career. He is named one of *Film Daily*'s "Famous Five" of the year. He ranks sixth in *Boxoffice* magazine's annual popularity poll (Paul Newman is first). He gets a second Golden Globe. In October, 1969, he is named Star of the Year by NATO, the National Association of Theater Owners. Accepting the award, he says, "This is the end of an era, the beginning of the end of movie stars."

It is also the end of his six-picture Solar deal with Warner Brothers. After *Bullitt* was finished, but before it was released, studio brass were screaming bloody murder about the picture's $200,000 budget override. At that point they flatly pulled out of the contract and canceled any future projects. Ah, but that was prior to the film's huge and unexpected success. McQueen thinks it's very funny that now that the picture has made a fortune, Warners wants him back. Too late: he's already split, locking the door behind him.

But what is he going to do now?

Japanese poster art for *Bullitt.*

The book's Boon: "Tough, faithful, brave, completely unreliable, six feet four inches tall, two hundred and forty pounds, with the mentality of a child." McQueen loves him. (All pictures copyright © 1969 by Cinema Center Films)

The Reivers

NATIONAL GENERAL, 1969

CREDITS

Director, *Mark Rydell*; producer, *Irving Ravetch*; executive producer, *Robert Relyea*; screenplay, *Ravetch, Harriet Frank, Jr.*, from the novel by *William Faulkner*; photographer, *Richard Moore* (Technicolor, Panavision); editor, *Thomas Stanford*; art directors, *Charles Bailey, Joel Schiller*; music, *John Williams*; casting, *Lynn Stalmaster*; costumes, *Theadora Van Runkle.*

CAST

Boon Hogganbeck *(STEVE McQUEEN)*, Corrie *(Sharon Farrell)*, Boss *(Will Geer)*, Ned Mc-Caslin *(Rupert Crosse)*, Lucius McCaslin (introducing *Mitch Vogel)*, Narrator *(Burgess Meredith)*, Sheriff Butch Lovemaiden *(Clifton James)*, Uncle Possum *(Juano Hernandez)*, Dr. Peabody *(Dub Taylor)*, Alison McCaslin *(Allyn Ann McLerie)*, Hannah (introducing *Diane Shalet)*, Phoebe *(Diane Ladd)*, Sally *(Ellen Geer).*

LOCATIONS: Carrolltown, Mississippi; Walt Disney Ranch, California.
A Solar Production of a Cinema Center Picture for National General release.

154

McQueen broadly overacts, going too far into Ham City at times, but the prevailing mood is one of great lovable rambunctiousness that overcomes his self-indulgence.

The other star of the movie: a 1905 lemon-colored Winton Flyer, now on display at Movie World in Buena Park, California, after being in McQueen's personal collection for a while.

A publicity shot of Sharon Farrell. Her golden-hearted hooker isn't nearly as tough as this picture pretends.

MPAA rating: M.
Opened December 25, 1969 (111 minutes).

REVIEWS

"A decent adaptation, with a lot of conventional good humor taken almost word-for-word from the book. However, casting McQueen as Boon automatically gives the character an inappropriate tool and shifts the film's attention from its nominal protagonist, young Lucius" (Vincent Canby, *New York Times*).

"It's fortunate McQueen is one of those rare modern actors whose presence carries the right kind of familiarity; he's ingratiating, and that's enough here" (Kathleen Carroll, *New York Daily News*).

"McQueen gives a lively, ribald characterization that suggests he will have a long career as a character actor after his sexy allure thins" (*Variety*).

It is 1969, the year of *Easy Rider*, the low-budget counterculture movie which has made tons of money and convinced Hollywood that the big-budget picture is dead.

McQueen believes it, too, and forms a partnership with Cinema Center, a fledgling producer and a subsidiary of CBS, which intends to hit the big time with little pictures.

Solar's first co-production with Cinema Center is *Adam at Six A.M.*, budgeted at $1.4 million. Modest but effective, it will nevertheless not make a cent, though Solar doesn't know that yet. The company has grown to a 25-person staff, which fills the third floor of an office building at Ventura and Radford, right across the street from the old Republic Studios. The billing reads McQueen as president, Robert Relyea as executive producer, and Jack Reddish, the production manager on *Bullitt*, as producer. Together, they package two McQueen-starrers for Cinema Center, *The Reivers* and *Le Mans*, with National General set to distribute.

The Reivers is based on William Faulkner's last novel, the book that finally got him the Pulitzer Prize, awarded posthumously. He had died in July of 1962, a month after its publication. It was not regarded as his usual masterful work, though it was set, as was most of his fiction, in the venerable old town of Jefferson, in Yoknapatawpha County, Mississippi. Far

Will Geer, still several years away from playing Grandpa Walton on CBS-TV, does an elegant job of playing the Southern gentleman incarnate, and has this remarkable scene with Mitch Vogel near the end of the movie.

Rupert Crosse, as McQueen's sidekick, has a fine, undemeaning role which very nearly went to Richard Pryor.

from being a Faulkner classic, the book still had a rich, mellow air about it, the work of a man looking fondly back upon an era that had never existed. Its humanitarianism and writer's craft counterbalanced the sentimentality.

The week it was published, theatrical producer David Merrick optioned the novel for long-range consideration as a Broadway musical. Six years later, McQueen picks up the option, intending to adapt it into a vehicle for himself. It goes to Cinema Center with a guarantee of location shooting which McQueen, like his mentor Sturges, considers absolutely necessary for maintaining the feel of the book. He's happily anticipating playing his first character role, the novel's Boon Hogganbeck, even though he isn't the book's focal character.

McQueen wants the best on the project, as always, and barters for old friend Mark Rydell.

Family portrait: child, child, woman.

As screenwriters he gets Faulkner specialists, husband-and-wife writing team Irving Ravetch and Harriet Frank, Jr., who had more or less successfully brought *The Sound and the Fury* to the screen in 1959 for director Martin Ritt. They had also created *The Long Hot Summer* with Paul Newman from *The Hamlet* in Faulkner's Snopes trilogy. Most importantly, they had received an Oscar for their screenplay for *Hud.*

Very funny sequence featuring mud, car, and movie star.

The picture is shot at Carrolltown, Mississippi, with its racing sequence filmed at the Walt Disney Ranch in California and interiors completed at CBS Studio Center in Hollywood.

The Reivers, as film, turns out to be an extremely likable piece, photographed by Richard Moore with a great expressive feel for this amber-tinted era. Only Burgess Meredith's off-camera narration, as the grown-up version of the 11-year-old protagonist (played by Mitch Vogel, in his time one of the few child actors who neither cloys nor irritates) really adheres to the Faulkner text. The rest of the picture keeps to the spirit of the book rather than to the letter.

The best moment comes near the end, as the boy wins a horse-race composed of slow-motion and dissolves, one of the loveliest cinematic set-pieces of the sixties. As Meredith's line goes, "It took me completely, skin, blood, bowels, bones and memory—more people watched me that day than I've ever seen. It was a fleeting moment of glory, a glory which could not last, but while it did it was the best game of all."

The only problem with the picture, truthfully, is its point of view. The book is about the boy, but the movie is about Boon. The picture is best when it tries to emulate a child's inno-

cent eye, but McQueen is the star and his presence just naturally pulls the attention his way.

And McQueen does a lot to deserve that attention. His entrance is in close-up, as he runs out of a house, buttoning his shirt, yanking a yellow rose off a bush as he runs. Craggy, countrified, his wheatlike hair longish (for him), his is a genuine character actor's part overblown into a star's role, but sweet and effective anyway.

And who would deny Steve McQueen a kiss, even in a William Faulkner comedy.

160

Off-camera, things are not so sweet. Former friend Rydell: "He was hard and he could be mean and he did have me with my back to the wall sometimes." When McQueen stayed pouting in his trailer, Rydell analyzes, "He wanted to feel that nothing could happen without him. He was an entirely instinctive actor. He never learned his lines, and after one, or at the most two, takes, he wasn't any good."

There are Oscar nods—not in McQueen's direction (he's not surprised) but to co-star Rupert Crosse, who receives a Best Supporting Actor nomination, but who loses to Gig Young's downbeat performance in *They Shoot Horses, Don't They?* John Williams's exquisite, Copland-like score is passed over in favor of Burt Bacharach's flashy anachronistic work for *Butch Cassidy and the Sundance Kid.*

In the end, McQueen decides he doesn't like the picture because he doesn't like himself in comedy. When will he learn?

Much of the movie is quite gently about sex, only an M rating's worth.

Le Mans

National General, 1971

CREDITS

Screenplay, director, *Lee H. Katzin;* producer, *Jack N. Reddish;* executive producer, *Robert Relyea;* associate producer, *Alan Levine;* photographers, *Robert B. Hauser, Rene Guissart, Jr.* (Deluxe Color, Panavision, Stereophonic Sound); editors, *Don Ernst, John Woodcock, Ghislaine Des Jonqueres;* production design, *Phil Abramson;* visual design, *Nikita Knatz;* music, *Michel Legrand;* costumes, *Ray Summers.*

CAST

Michael Delaney *(STEVE McQUEEN)*, Erich Stahler *(Siegfried Rauch)*, Lisa Belgetti *(Elga Anderson)*, David Townsend *(Ronald Leigh-Hunt)*, Johann Ritter *(Fred Haltiner)*, Claude Aurac *(Luc Merenda)*, and 45 Le Mans drivers.

LOCATIONS: Le Mans Race Track, France.
A Solar Production of a Cinema Center Picture for National General release.
SHOOTING TITLES: *The Cruel Sport, Day of the Champions, Day of the Champion, The 24 Hours of Le Mans.*
MPAA rating: G.
Opened June 23, 1971 (106 minutes).

REVIEWS

"The picture is a bore" (Howard Thompson, *New York Times*).

"Appears to be an excuse for Steve McQueen to indulge his passion for auto racing. There is no attempt at characterization. The dialogue is dreadful" (Kathleen Carroll, *New York Daily News*).

"Steve McQueen's style of glacial cool has been perfected close to the point of impenetrable mannerism. He only stands in front of the camera and allows himself to be photographed. Occasionally, his lips will twitch into that shy, strong, ironic half-smile he has made his trademark. In really grandiose scenes he may make a gesture. He might even wave. But only under pressure. McQueen is still potentially a good movie actor, but he needs someone to loosen him up, make him play a part, not pose for it. He has surrounded himself with the sort of second-rate production talent that offers no

Director Lee Katzin readies a shot as gendarmes protect McQueen (inside the Porsche) from the curious. (All pictures copyright © 1971 by Cinema Center Films)

protest to his rampant self-indulgence" (Jay Cocks, *Time*).

"You can't hear the words for the noise, you can't follow the action for the speed. But you can sit back and feel distinctly stirred" (Dilys Powell, *London Sunday Times*).

What a bizarre year 1969 is turning out to be. McQueen has one flop period comedy under his belt. He's getting more flack than ever from Neile about his reckless, but so far wreckless, racing. After the Tate-Lo Bianca murders, his name is published in the newspaper as being part of a Manson death list, alongside the Burtons and Frank Sinatra. And, he is told, he has made Nixon's notorious Enemies List, even though he is as apolitical a being as has ever lived.

What else is there to do but drive?

In his ongoing desire to bring a great race-track story to the screen, McQueen and James Garner travel to Mexico to appear as drivers, not actors, in the movie version of the Mexican 1000 road race.

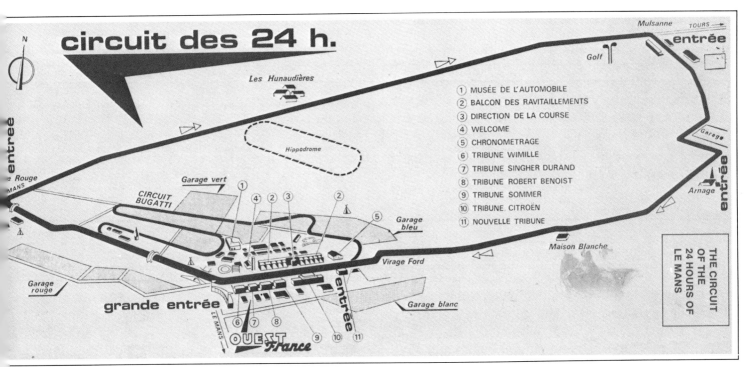

The Le Mans circuit.

163

McQueen strikes a stance next to his Porsche 917.

164

Bolting a Panavision camera in place for an arresting POV shot. McQueen is back left.

The Image film is shot November, 1969, but McQueen and Garner quit after three weeks, sick of the attitude of unprofessionalism pervading the production. They sue to remove their names from the film, *Mexican 1000*, and as a result it is never finished and never released.

The racing bug is still there, though, and McQueen continues to think about his fantasy: to create a motion picture based in racing. It would combine his two greatest loves. It is irresistible. It will rank with the impact Howard Hawks' *The Crowd Roars* had on audiences in 1932. This, of course, will be larger, all-encompassing, a definitive portrait of all the major tracks of the world.

That idea will eventually be forced through depressing circumstances to focus on a single track, and cause McQueen to look back on this, his dearest hope, as "a bloodbath."

In 1965, McQueen, John Sturges, and John Frankenheimer jointly announce they have

Siegfried Rauch and Elga Anderson provide minimal support (blame the script) as rival and lover.

165

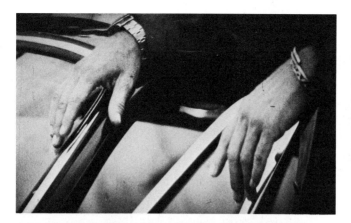

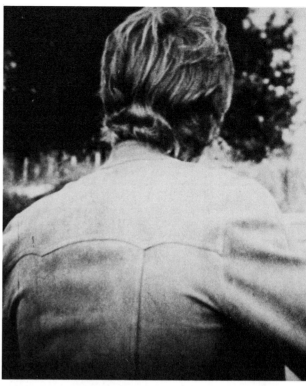

The star's megalomaniacal entrance: his face is hidden behind windshield reflections, and when he gets out of his car, the camera studies the back of his head, then swivels around in tight close-up, a full 180 degrees, slowly, slowly, until McQueen's face comes into full view. The process is reverential.

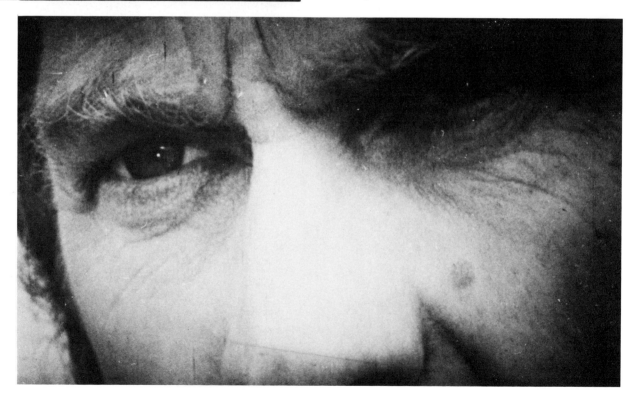

McQueen, here in helmet and fire mask, doesn't speak for the first 40 minutes, building his character through the applause he receives from the stands.

acquired the rights to film Robert Daley's racing book *The Cruel Sport.* Presumably, the fact that two directors are to work on the project is not an obstacle or an oversight. Perhaps one is to work more on the producing end. Maybe one will handle off-track scenes, the other direct the filming of the actual racing scenes. Each man has an excellent track record, too: Sturges as the leading visual action director whom McQueen trusts implicitly to handle him correctly; and Frankenheimer, whose recent filmography includes the impressive *Seven Days in May, The Manchurian Candidate,* and *The Train.*

But the three men are unable to come up with one conception for the picture's visualization that they all can agree on, and the triumvirate splits up into two units, with Frankenheimer going his own way, leaving McQueen and Sturges to work on their own.

However, Frankenheimer also takes with him his portion of the rights to the source book, and announces that he is planning a racing production under the title *The Cruel Sport.* Its option is picked up by MGM, though at this point it is unknown what direction the project will take. Vindictively, Sturges and McQueen also retain *The Cruel Sport* as their title, resulting in two simultaneous productions being announced under the same title by separate factions. Each comes to realize the foolhardiness of their strongly felt obstinacy. So while Frankenheimer retitles his *Grand Prix,* McQueen and Sturges call theirs *Day of the Champions.*

Now, the original idea has been to film a movie about all the world's significant racing events. Frankenheimer has narrowed his to a single race, leaving everything else seemingly wide open for McQueen and Sturges. That is

167

Criticism that McQueen just stands there and lets himself be photographed does seem valid.

It is the photography that is the major point of interest. It's gorgeous stuff, with a lot of late-sixties typically tightly held telephoto shots and sudden zoom-ins. Panavision close-ups with sudden pullbacks are common, and odd angles and forced perspective are everywhere.

not to be. Keeping the *Day of the Champions* title, McQueen and Sturges start scouting European locations for track shooting, only to discover Frankenheimer has picked up exclusive rights to most of the prestigious sites. McQueen and Sturges' search narrows to tracks in England and France, hoping to develop an idea whereby a single driver might be traced as he drives many of the significant courses. With that fresh idea, the title is shortened by a single letter to *Day of the Champion.*

By March, 1965, Edward Anhalt has been announced as the film's screenwriter. Later that year, Jackie Stewart is its scheduled star, with Stirling Moss as technical advisor. And the film is set to be distributed by Warner Brothers. In preparation for the film, McQueen, with Sturges' advice and guidance, shoots 35,000 feet of footage of the 1965 Le Mans competition, intending to use the location shots for the eventual film. All seems set.

Principal photography is supposed to begin on July 5, 1966, at Germany's Nurburgring track, but McQueen is on location in the Orient for *The Sand Pebbles,* having encountered demoralizing production delays from the torrential rain and the resulting riots. Thus he is unable to meet Warners' shooting schedule, due to prior contractual obligations. Filming in Taiwan and Hong Kong has run well past the time when McQueen wants to be on hand to shoot the summer races, so Warners shelves the project until the next year.

In April, 1967, however, trade papers indicate *Day of the Champion* will be out sometime in 1968. And then Warners decides to drop the project, because they'd only stayed with it if it could beat out Metro's *Grand Prix* to the screen. Furthermore, says Warners, *Day*'s intimately detailed diary of a driver cannot hope to compete critically and financially with Frankenheimer's hard-ticket road-show Cinerama version with full stereo and

Spectacular crash footage is shot and edited to give the dreamlike experience of unexpected disaster. Especially good is the stuntman's slow-motion trajectory from his flaming vehicle.

stunning special effects. It might not be the same kind of picture, they agree, but the public cannot be educated to know that. So all McQueen's hopes, as well as his six miles of Le Mans footage, find themselves looking for a distributor.

With Sturges, McQueen revamps the concept and turns it into *Le Mans*, a portrait of a single race that will have special box-office value by having McQueen himself drive in the actual race, partnered by Peter Revson. He will play himself, and the film will be more a documentary about the race and the racers than a study of a single driver's sojourn around Europe's tracks. With the new approach in hand, McQueen goes to Cinema Center, which had backed *The Reivers*, hoping to catch a distributor in its outlet, National General.

But Cinema Center doesn't want a documentary. They want a story, danger, a rivalry, a love interest, all the elements of fiction feature-making for the entertainment market. They make it clear that the picture won't be made without the romance, especially, and superimpose at their discretion a lifeless script over McQueen's protests.

Sturges has vanished by this time, fed up with the whole thing, arguing with McQueen constantly over what shape the film should take. McQueen, one of the original troika that had proposed the spectacular idea, is now alone in his determination to bring it to the screen.

He has become obsessive. Neile tries dragging him away to Morocco to forget, but he is on the phone constantly. She doesn't like him doing a racing film anyway, and she feels he's taking the project much too personally.

Backed by Cinema Center, whatever their unhappy terms, McQueen hits still another obstacle. He can't compete in the race if a fictional script is to be the method of presentation for the film, retitled yet again: *The 24 Hours of Le Mans.* His bitterness increases as he returns to the track in 1969 and 1970 for each year's race to capture footage in which "Michael Delaney" (McQueen's role) will compete. But since McQueen is not in the race, the track has to be secured later in the summer of 1970 to set up expensive simulations of the real race yet to be run.

McQueen and his executive producer, Robert Relyea, take over the circuit for 12 weeks, using 19 cameras spread over the course and a Porsche 908 equipped with three cameras to shoot POV, both for the simulation and for the actual race. Tracking car is a GT-40 Ford. Additionally, a million dollars' worth of vehicles are bought or leased, including three Porsche 917's valued at $70,000 each and four Ferrari 512's ($55,000 apiece). McQueen grabs one of the Porsches, equipped with a 600hp engine, as his screen car. The mock-up includes real drivers from the race, and the crew includes a man who realistically squashes bugs against the windshields.

From June to November, 1970, McQueen and replacement director Lee H. Katzin run through an incredible 450,000 feet of film, which is then edited down into showable form over a six-month cutting-room period. Katzin,

Distributor National General tries three different ad campaigns to sell the picture. Nothing works.

a Harvard man lately given to TV work, sees his job clearly: he must always console McQueen, soothe the other drivers' ruffled feathers, and make a movie out of this two-year debacle.

Costs have risen to a whopping $6 million. McQueen has produced his own runaway. "It's big, it's bad, and it's expensive," he tells *Playboy.* "I enjoy the fact that we're playing for big marbles. I'm a filmmaker; I feel very strongly about not compromising the film for a business reason. I enjoy the spooky feeling of having it all on my back, but I don't like anyone fucking with my head while I'm doing it."

Under the title *Le Mans,* the completed film opens in June, 1971, in New York. Six years, millions of dollars, all those heartaches, personal sacrifices, and McQueen's aching willpower have culminated in this moment. But *Time* calls it "Petit Prix." Their review is typical. Warner Brothers' premonition has been proven right, and although critics who like it really like it, the script is heartily condemned as a star's self-serving excuse to make himself an idol at any price. No one in the media knows the truth.

The fictional element really isn't so bad. Yes, it's soap opera, but it's handled in an almost completely visual way. Not a single word of actual dialog is heard during the first half-hour, yet we know exactly what's going on, practically through image alone and from public address information, the loudspeaker becoming a character just as in Robert Altman's *M*A*S*H.* Elsewhere the complications are laconic, and Cinema Center's fictional overlay is not quite realized.

But who cares? The splendid visuals are the film's glorious *raison d'etre.* The race footage is professional, knowledgeable, and exciting, edited with an razor-sharp blade. The crashes are thrilling, captured with 14 cameras, three of them running in slow-motion. And the POV shots are dazzling, like the one that reveals the horror of a windshield instantly transformed into a deadly spider's web while you watch.

All in all, a worthy film now buried because it was a commercial failure, unaided even by visual designer Nikita Knatz' documentary *Le Mans and the Man McQueen.* The star does not consider it a bomb: he has done what he wanted to do. He's just the only person who knows it.

On Any Sunday

Bikers Mert Lawwill, Malcolm Smith, and Steve McQueen. (All pictures copyright © 1971 by Cinema 5).

CINEMA 5, 1971

CREDITS

Producer-director-narrator, *Bruce Brown;* photographers, *Bob Bagley* and 11 more (Technicolor); editor, *Don Shoemaker;* opticals, titles, Cinema Research; production manager, *Bob Bagley.*

PARTICIPANTS:

STEVE McQUEEN, *Mert Lawwill, Malcolm Smith, Gene Romero, Jim Rice, Dick Mann, Whitey Martino,* etc.

EVENTS:

Mert Lawwill segment; Moto-Cross*; Malcolm Smith segment; International Six-Day Trials, El Escorial, Spain; Grand Prix, Elsinore, California*; Drag-racing; Ice-racing, Quebec; Bonneville Salt Flats, Utah; Sacramento segment; Widowmaker Hill Climb, Utah; Trials Riders; Desert racing, Mojave Desert*; Conclusion—cow-trailing.*

Produced in association with Solar Productions.

(*indicates McQueen sequence)

MPAA rating: G.
Opened July 28, 1971 (89 minutes).

REVIEWS

"An exciting documentary of one of the most dangerous of all sports. McQueen's prowess as a racer is demonstrated time and again and his name should spark interest in a film that alone stands as a spectacular piece of filmmaking" *(Variety).*

"A distinctly unconvincing celebration of motorcycle racing. Brown is at pains to include every conceivable cliché of documentary film-making. There is plenty of slow motion, a rash of feeble jokes, and a musical score that sounds like 'The Glory of Tupperware' " (Jay Cocks, *Time).*

One of the more obscure pictures of McQueen's career is quite personal, his participation in Bruce Brown's motorcycle documentary *On Any Sunday.*

McQueen and Brown have been talking about doing the picture since 1969. By mid-1970, McQueen's importance in the industry is such that he makes $500,000 per year salary from Solar as president of the company (the

president of the United States only makes $100,000 annually). Plus he makes that much or better from the studio distributing his current film. Plus he always has a percentage of the film's gross. He can now pay for his own vehicles. Quietly.

So McQueen agrees to finance the film for a whispery, wispy $300,000 in exchange for his appearance in it. His terms; he must be presented as a serious figure in bike-racing, a sober competitor who is respected by his two-wheeler peers. His motives: to gain public acceptance as something more than a movie star, and to do on a small scale for bikes what he has done for auto racing in *Le Mans*.

The motorcycle movie has stayed with him like a pet project all through the rigors of *Le Mans*. Now he is ready to tackle it, but only with Brown, who has made a good industry name for himself with his *Endless Summer* surfing documentary. Together they seek to create a 16mm ode to the bike. They enter the project with idealism, and come out financial winners.

Brown employs 12 cinematographers, including himself, to travel all over America and

Europe, covering 10,000 miles in two years, from Spain to California.

Several sequences feature McQueen. He's in the moto-cross sequence that opens the movie, in which Brown says that McQueen is risking "A million-dollar body. No movie actor at the starting line, he's 100 percent motorcycle rider." At the 1970 Lake Elsinore Grand Prix, Brown says Steve "won the respect of other riders, who didn't realize how good a rider he was." McQueen finishes tenth out of 500 riders. A desert racing sequence features some 2000 hard riders who tear across 100 miles of the worst the land has to offer. Brown carefully notes that McQueen is ranked the # 11 desert racer. Finally, professionals Mert Lawwill and Malcolm Smith, who have the most footage and the finest reputations, join McQueen in a finale of cow-trailing and beach-riding.

Despite McQueen's presence, the film never makes it above glorified home-movie, due largely to Brown's "Gee whiz" narration. It's the kind of documentary where you see a crash and Brown tells you you've seen a crash. Riders plow through guard rails, brush the dust off and go back to the race in a devastating por-

(*Pages 176-181*) Bruce Brown biker visions.

trayal of nerve and stupidity. Brown records these hazards but never questions them. He also glamorizes crashes with ultra slow-motion, lyrical dissolves, hazy telephoto shots, which worked in *Le Mans* because it was fiction, but which shock here because it is documentary. The danger is romanticized.

Moral issues aside, the sheer pictorial imagery (best appreciated with the sound off) succeeds as itself. Like a lap race, shot POV looking over the handlebars at 160 mph. Like showing the clear plastic strips riders tape to their visors to tear off one by one as dirt and insects obscure their vision. Like the grinding away of mere grams from machine parts in a tooling shop to cut the bike's weight by precious ounces. Like the mechanics of the special skid boot designed for the left foot.

In sum, the film pretty much does what McQueen has intended. He counts it a success when $10 million in domestic rentals validates his involvement. He picks up more profits in 1974, thanks to a $3 million distribution deal offered by Yamaha, which has no bikes in the picture. They just think it's good PR. But he has no interest or participation in a 1979 sequel offered by Inter Planetary Pictures. By then, his mind is elsewhere.

McQueen in a candid moment with Lawwill.

182

Junior Bonner

ABC-CINERAMA, 1972

CREDITS

Director, *Sam Peckinpah;* producer, *Joe Wizan;* associate producer, *Mickey Borofsky;* screenplay, *Jeb Rosebrook;* photographer, *Lucien Ballard* (Movielab Color, Todd-AO 35); editor, *Robert Wolf;* art director, *Edward S. Haworth;* music, *Jerry Fielding;* casting, *Lynn Stalmaster;* costumes, *Eddie Armand;* technical advisor, *Casey Tibbs.*

CAST

Junior Bonner *(STEVE McQUEEN),* Ace Bonner *(Robert Preston),* Elvira Bonner *(Ida Lupino),* Curly Bonner *(Joe Don Baker),* Charmagne *(Barbara Leigh),* Ruth Bonner *(Mary Murphy),* Buck Roan *(Ben Johnson),* Tim Bonner *(Matthew Peckinpah),* Singer *(Rod Hart).*

LOCATIONS: Prescott, Arizona.
A Solar Production.
MPAA rating: PG.
Opened August 2, 1972 (103 minutes).

REVIEWS

"McQueen has a chance to do a lot of what he does so well: nothing much while he thinks

McQueen displays a better physical build than he has ever shown on screen.

Original sweat-stained ad art. (All pictures copyright © 1972 by ABC Pictures Corporation and Cinerama Releasing)

about some action that has happened or will. He keeps it all in focus with those steady blue eyes of his. A hero from the past, McQueen, as always, makes you believe it" (Archer Winsten, *New York Post*).
"A nice, loose, easy-going rodeo picture. McQueen has met with a role that fits him like a glove" (Kathleen Carroll, *New York Daily News*).
"For those of us who have come to expect (or

fear) that each new Sam Peckinpah film will be a new bloodbath, this comes as a pleasant surprise, a reminder of milder, gentler films" (John Russell Taylor, *London Times*).

The part is the thing. He is very disappointed when his ally David Foster buys the book *The Presbyterian Church Wager* and offers the lead to Warren Beatty instead of to himself. McQueen would have enjoyed playing the doomed but affable Western hero, but Beatty accepts the role in the now retitled *McCabe and Mrs. Miller.*

In an effort, then, to maintain greater control over the selection of his material, McQueen joins First Artists in March, 1971. It is something unique in the industry, an independent producing company formed by the biggest box-office stars of the day. He, as a potent film force, is the equal of partners Barbra Streisand, Paul Newman, Sidney Poitier and, eventually, Dustin Hoffman. With the new company, he will begin exercising practically complete control over the selection, conception, and execution of special properties.

He begins his search for a suitable vehicle, but the search is interrupted in June when Neile petitions for divorce after 14 years of marriage. She has left him, she says, for only one reason: his dangerous professional driving career. "Some men drink," she tells a reporter. "Steve races."

McQueen has seen it coming for years, but it is still a shock, especially because it is she who has filed against him, not the other way around, as he had more or less expected. He has no choice but to let her go through with it. In truth, he doesn't even seem all that upset by the move, though the remorse he feels is nowhere near what he shows.

The following March 14, 1972, it will become final in Santa Monica court, with Neile receiving a million-dollar settlement. She retains custody of 12-year-old Terri and 11-year-old Chad, and receives an additional $500,000 per year alimony and child support for the next ten

McQueen opens the film with a full-screen close-up and its first line: "Maybe I oughta take up another line of work." He drives a white Cadillac convertible in homage to *Hud.*

years. The four former family members remain friendly. There is no bitterness; the time for that has long passed.

While all of this is in the works, McQueen keeps looking for the right property and thinks he has found it in November, 1971. He announces that First Artists will produce and National General distribute *American Flag*, from a novel by rugged storyteller Elmore Leonard. The author has already completed a script, at the same time that he is finishing *Joe Kidd* for Clint Eastwood. This Western mining saga is to be made under the banner of Astral Productions International, an independent producing company Solar has acquired. Solar itself remains outside First Artists' domain.

First Artists, though, is beginning to do a lot less than what McQueen had gone into it thinking it would be. What had begun as the most stellar assemblage of moviedom's personages since Chaplin, Pickford, Fairbanks, and Griffith created United Artists in 1919 now looks like just another tax-shelter operation. Certainly not a production company headed by people who care deeply about total control of their movies. The pictures it has released are tame: Streisand's *Up the Sandbox*, Newman's *Pocket Money*, Poitier's *Buck and the Preacher*. They do only fair box-office, and the laissez-faire board of directors does not seem interested in the active pursuit of hot deals.

Thus McQueen turns his attentions to another offer. He chooses to do *Junior Bonner*, a tough but lyrical look at the new West to be directed by Sam Peckinpah.

McQueen had almost worked with Peckinpah on *The Cincinnati Kid*. But when the stubborn maverick director had insisted on a then-forbidden female nude scene, he was pink-slipped and shown the door by Metro. Now, though, he is a major industry figure to reckon with, mostly because of *The Wild Bunch*, which has ended one chapter on the Hollywood Western and begun another. Embodiments of his theme of the Western man who finds himself a relic have in the past included Randolph Scott, Joel McCrea, William Holden, Robert Ryan, Ernest Borgnine, and Ben Johnson. McQueen is just about to try to join their ranks.

Peckinpah sets his tale during Prescott, Arizona's Frontier Days celebration, an annual

event heralding in loud and gaudy Western fashion the brief return of an old way of life. In this setting he places the family Bonner, like the town festival a graying institution. The conflict of the family having to face modern times appears most literally in the juxtaposition of old and new Wests as bulldozers tear up the ancestral homestead. Peckinpah, however, deals with the family realistically. When Junior returns to Prescott to see his family, for instance, he finds his parents have split up.

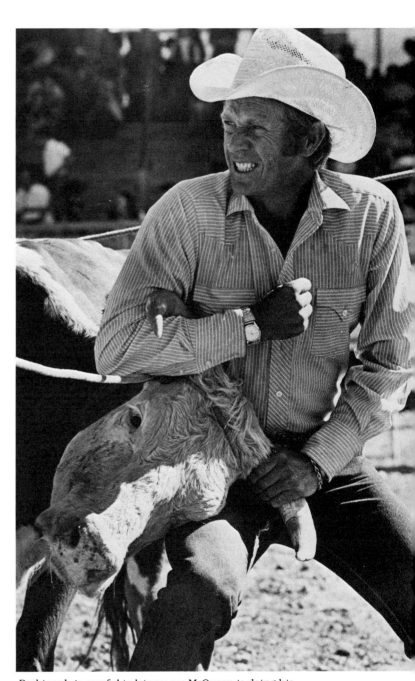

McQueen (shown here with Robert Preston) has a hard time training to do the rodeo stunts, calling it the most difficult physical work of his career.

Peckinpah is careful to let you see McQueen is doing his own stuntwork, presenting action sequences in slow-motion to prove there are no doubles, whom both director and star scorn. In 1977 McQueen will be made an honorary member of the Stuntman's Association of Motion Pictures in recognition of this dedication.

What is most surprising about the film, when it opens in August, 1972, is its astonishing lack of violence. It is far less brutally macho than Peckinpah is always expected to be, though it is still a ritual celebration of maleness. Totems include boozing, barroom-brawling, blonde-baiting, and bronco-busting. There is plenty of the expected in the rodeo arena, where cameras capture the agony of each event in Peckinpah's trademark slow-motion, but no longer does Peckinpah seem hypnotized by the

sight of a .45 slug tearing through a human body. He actually seems more intent on exploring relationships. And he does not subvert his wistfulness for a older times to a hazy, nostalgic tone. His story is realistic sentimentality, a dusty opus with saddle sores, much like his *Ballad of Cable Hogue.*

But the movie does not perform well at the box-office. One reason is that all of a sudden the rodeo picture is trendy. Cliff Robertson has written, directed, and starred as not-so-bright *J.W. Coop,* picking up wide praise for his efforts. McQueen honcho James Coburn has been the similarly aging rodeo star of *The Honkers,* actor Steve Ihnat's only film as a director before his unexpected death. And Richard Widmark is soon to be on hand as—surprise!—an over-the-hill calf-roper in *When the Legends Die.*

Starring in his first film in nine years is stalwart Robert Preston, whose performance some critics find his best ever.

188

McQueen (barechested at least once in every movie) with "mother" Ida Lupino, a well-known actress and little-known director who is just coming into vogue from new interest in women's studies. "Brother" Joe Don Baker is literally just weeks away from stardom in his *Walking Tall* vigilante saga.

Further, of the 36 films ABC Pictures is making, an incredible 30 of them go red, including *Junior Bonner,* which loses $3 million. McQueen has been convinced from the beginning that ABC's marketing strategy would be wrong, that the film should open small and be allowed to build. When the movie dies, it is a curious and unfortunate confirmation of his business sense.

On the bright side, however, McQueen has found in Peckinpah a new compadre, someone who understands his image and who can create therefrom. It is not to be their only film together.

Ben Johnson, having copped his first Oscar for *The Last Picture Show* just as *Junior Bonner* is going before the camera, makes his role a kind of Greek chorus in spurs, a smalltime living legend from Amarillo, Texas, who stands for the last of the vanished West. Shown here in rare form with Sandra Deel.

The Prescott Frontier Days fiesta serves as the movie's atmospheric backdrop, with Preston's character symbolically riding in the parade between the Indians and the American flag, between the Old West and the New. McQueen makes Preston a fantasy father-figure, placing in Preston's mouth his own oft-mentioned dream of dropping his whole life and moving to Australia.

189

The Getaway

NATIONAL GENERAL, 1972

The picture is sold by word-of-mouth, as National General's publicity mill inveigles audiences into seeing the screen's hot new love team, only to disappoint them with an apathetic rendering of the wife who willingly betrays her husband for a stake in the loot. (All pictures copyright © 1972 by National General Pictures Corporation)

CREDITS

Director, *Sam Peckinpah;* producers, *David Foster, Mitchell Brower;* screenplay, *Walter Hill,* from the novel by *Jim Thompson;* photographer, *Lucien Ballard* (Technicolor, Todd-AO 35); editor, *Robert Wolf;* art directors, *Ted Haworth, Angelo Graham;* music, *Quincy Jones;* musical voices, *Don Elliott;* harmonica solos, *Toots Thielemans;* costumes, *Ray Summers.*

CAST

Carter "Doc" McCoy *(STEVE McQUEEN),* Carol Ainsley McCoy *(Ali MacGraw),* Jack Benyon *(Ben Johnson),* Fran Clinton *(Sally Struthers),* Rudy Butler *(Al Lettieri),* Cowboy *(Slim Pickens),* Thief *(Richard Bright),* Harold Clinton *(Jack Dodson),* Laughlin *(Dub Taylor),* Frank Jackson *(Bo Hopkins).*

LOCATIONS: Huntsville, San Antonio and El Paso, Texas.
A First Artists-Solar Production.
MPAA rating: PG.
Opened December 19, 1972 (122 minutes).

REVIEWS

"The picture's bewildering con is that it makes the pair such lovely, decent gangsters that they can stroll off into the sunset with their satchel stuffed with money as if they'd just met over a malted at the corner drugstore. As for McQueen and MacGraw, they strike no sparks on the screen. (They don't even look right together; her head is bigger than his). His low-key professionalism is turning into minimal acting, and is indistinguishable from the blahs, while she is certainly the primmest, smuggest gangster's moll of all time" (Pauline Kael, *The New Yorker*).

"I suspect MacGraw may turn out to be quite a subtle actress with a lot of staying power" (George Melly, *The Observer*).

"If 'The Getaway' had just rolled off the studio assembly line, the work of a competent craftsman, it could easily have been passed over and forgotten. It is, however, the work of a major American film artist. Peckinpah is pushing his privileges too far" (Jay Cocks, *Time*).

Alone now for the first time since the mid-fifties, McQueen throws himself into his work.

Getting lazier and lazier as he makes more and more per picture, heaven for him is making a film every 18 months or so. When he does look seriously for work, however, he does so cautiously, going for character over action. Thus it is that he becomes enamored of *Roy Brightsword*, about a wildass Arkansas hillbilly who is tamed by a Jewish social worker during the Depression.

First Artists' board, though, turns it down and the property is returned to its author, actor Laurence Luckinbill, who is similarly unsuccessful in turning it into a vehicle for himself.

Turning elsewhere, McQueen has long wanted to play a good/bay guy, a Bogart kind of role, he says. His agent Mike Medavoy finds it in the form of a 25-cent paperback, a crime story by Jim Thompson called *The Getaway*, published in 1958 but set in the 40's. Looks perfect. But it will turn out to be a crazy and decisive turning point in McQueen's life. Of all the films thus far in his career, it is only this one which will most profoundly and directly reflect the pulsebeat of his private life.

It seems so easy to Medavoy and McQueen's trusted friend producer David Foster as they start to package the story, which is about one last job an ex-con and his duplicitous wife try to pull off. For director, young Peter Bogdanovich's name is mentioned. The men go to see his new film *The Last Picture Show* with Bogdanovich present. The screening is over at 4:00 p.m. A deal is made by 5:00. The leading lady will most likely be Dyan Cannon, Angie Dickinson, or Farrah Fawcett. Jack Palance is contacted to consider playing the villain. Jerry Fielding is already beginning to write the score. The script is coming from newcomer Walter Hill (who dedicates the screenplay to classic action director Raoul Walsh). He has updated the setting to contemporary Texas, and has kept all the action within the state's borders, unlike the novel. He's eliminated the book's near-

The wife conspires with the husband's enemy (Ben Johnson) all for a lot of silver and green. Johnson had just supplied an Oscar-winning performance as the endearing, enduring Sam the Lion in Bogdanovich's *The Last Picture Show*. Here he plays an icy Texas criminal/businessman in a film originally to have been directed by Bogdanovich.

191

surrealistic ending that finds the couple happy in a larger-than-life thieves' hideaway in Mexico. He has, however, maintained the Doc character's cold-blooded smile and sandy hair as tailor-made for McQueen. The last piece falls into place when Paramount indicates interest in distribution.

Now the madness begins. Bogdanovich decides he'd rather write as well as direct, and has the opportunity to do so at Warner Brothers with *What's Up, Doc?* He exits. As a replacement, McQueen indicates he has a personal preference for Sam Peckinpah, with whom he has just completed *Junior Bonner.* Medavoy and Foster agree immediately, as does Peckinpah. Peckinpah, however, wants to use Stella Stevens as the female lead, and dumps Palance. But Stevens is unavailable, and Palance replies with a $100,000 breach of contract suit (he will later drop the case because lawyers tell him his demands for excessive expenses and above-the-title billing hold no legal water without signed contracts).

Then Paramount places the project in turnaround, Hollywood protocol translating "thanks, but no thanks." It is offered to First Artists, which is willing to take over the film for a fee of nothing up front against 10 percent of the gross from the first dollar. The deal works out very well for McQueen, who agrees to 22½ percent of the net plus a substantial share in First Artists as his salary. Having First Artists pick it up also satisfies certain obligations between Solar and First Artists, to wit, that Solar, like the other partners' parent production companies, must provide First Artists with three films during the first five years of FA's existence. *The Getaway* is the first of those three, and it is set to be distributed by National General. Definitely. NG president Charles Boasberg is delighted, projecting a gross of at least $25 million on the picture.

So much for getting another director and another distributor. Now what about the dame?

Enter Ali MacGraw.

A Wellesley graduate and former model, she has debuted in 1968's *A Lovely Way to Die* in a bit part, followed by her first starring role in *Goodbye, Columbus.* The film that has made her a genuine household name, however, is the blockbuster tearjerker *Love Story,* produced by Robert Evans, Paramount's executive vice-

McQueen gets to drive, not unexpectedly, and here he ends the *de rigueur* car chase in his baby-blue Ford with a couple of explosions and a head-on collision with somebody's front porch.

McQueen is at the most violent he has ever been, armed with potent weapons like this .45 in this, his second film foray into the bank-robbery genre.

Never more raw than when toting a scattergun, ready to pump it into anyone who makes him mad. He plays the role as if letting out the accumulated rage of his 42 years.

president in charge of worldwide production. She is also Evans's wife.

While many columnists are contemptuous of MacGraw's seemingly easy entree into the motion picture industry, the truth is that she has had a bitch of a time getting people to take her seriously. Now, even though Paramount has dropped *The Getaway*, Evans, concerned for her professional well-being, encourages her to go for the gun moll's role to change her image. If Ali can gain a reputation as a serious actress, Evans will have a much better chance convincing Paramount that she's right for the studio's ritzy *The Great Gatsby*, which she very badly aches to do.

Still quite hesitant about the part, Ali goes to see Foster, who later says of the event, "Mike and [co-producer] Mitch Brower and I met with her and she was wonderful, the most wonderful woman I have ever met in my life besides my wife Jackie. We really did a number on ourselves. We could see the marquee: 'McQueen and MacGraw!' and we convinced ourselves we wanted to go for commercialism, not artistic quality. So we went with her." Her terms: $300,000 plus 7½ percent of the net. She also says she'd have preferred Warren Beatty or Robert Redford as her leading man, but McQueen will do. Anything is worth it, she figures, to get out of the *Love Story* trap.

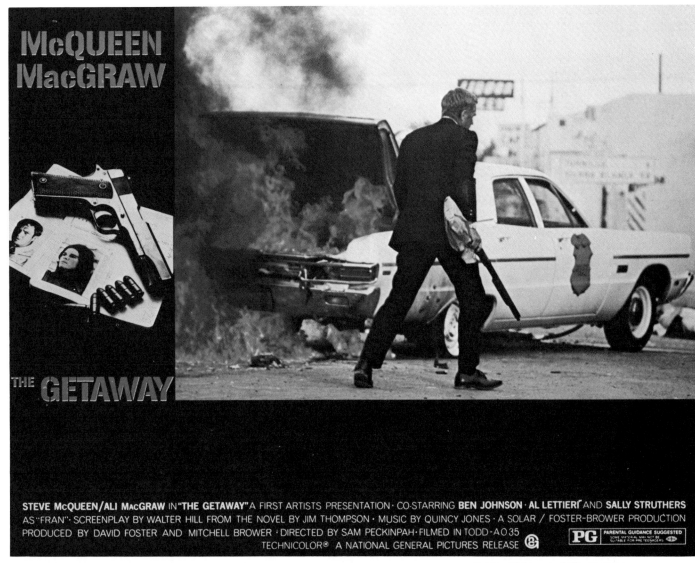

McQUEEN
MacGRAW

THE GETAWAY

STEVE McQUEEN/ALI MacGRAW IN "THE GETAWAY" A FIRST ARTISTS PRESENTATION · CO-STARRING **BEN JOHNSON** · **AL LETTIERI** AND **SALLY STRUTHERS** AS "FRAN". SCREENPLAY BY WALTER HILL FROM THE NOVEL BY JIM THOMPSON · MUSIC BY QUINCY JONES · A SOLAR / FOSTER-BROWER PRODUCTION PRODUCED BY DAVID FOSTER AND MITCHELL BROWER · DIRECTED BY SAM PECKINPAH · FILMED IN TODD-A0 35 TECHNICOLOR® A NATIONAL GENERAL PICTURES RELEASE

Original lobby card illustrating a scene McQueen has added to the script, in which he executes a Plymouth police car with his ever-ready scattergun, blowing it to slow-motion smithereens.

An interesting play with time in which a sequence showing McQueen and MacGraw plunging fully clothed into a pond is editorially constructed so that what we're watching might be fantasy, might be memory.

195

With the start of principal photography at Huntsville Prison in Texas on February 28, 1972, so ensues the romance between the two big Macs.

The movie is shot entirely on location, beginning at Huntsville for four days, then moving to San Antonio for six days, and finally to headquarters at El Paso for a hard five weeks.

The affair blossoms somewhere in the middle of it all, but onlookers ascribe it to the attraction the rough-hewn McQueen has for finishing-school product MacGraw. He's newly divorced, she's in Texas, a good century away from her sophisticated husband, and we all know about these location romances, don't we? Eventually she must face the repercussions caused by fan magazine leaks of the affair, and she returns to Evans. It looks good for a while, but it turns out to be only a game of cohabita-

Peckinpah directing behind the camera on location in Texas.

tion played for the public's benefit. McQueen, meanwhile, waits patiently on the sidelines for what he knows is the inevitable. He is cocksure. For unknown to cast and crew, to Peckinpah and Paramount, this publicity agent's dream stunt has turned out to be the real damn thing.

With the shoot completed, McQueen takes almost full control of the picture's shape. He always has, but he's been a lot feistier about it on this picture than previously. He's behaved so authoritatively on the set that when he gets the flu, an irritated crew must take it to a vote, 70 to 49, to decide whether or not to send him a get-well-card. Now he pulls the picture out of Peckinpah's hands with National General's sanction, and re-edits it to the point where Peckinpah, as is his norm, disowns the final cut. Finally, Foster, acting on McQueen's go-ahead, cans Jerry Fielding's long-finished score and replaces it with a new one by Quincy Jones.

Supporting actor Al Lettieri is an especially vicious villain.

196

Ad art (unwisely) stresses the romantic over the actionful.

The movie's primary location, El Paso's Hotel Laughlin, is demolished soon after to make room for a new Sheraton.

McQueen highly approves of the final product. It is his first big hit since *Bullitt,* four years and four movies prior.

Another problem encountered in post-production is the budget. There has been a $300,000 overrun, and since First Artists always includes a proviso that it finances only to the $3 million mark, the excess must somehow be dealt with. MacGraw becomes the heroine of the moment when she agrees to take the profits from the German release of *The Getaway,* trimming the budget back down to everyone's satisfaction.

Done at last, the tortuously created picture comes off as minor Peckinpah, long on violence and short on character. There are several taut scenes, including a celebrated, if overextended garbage sequence wherein McQueen and MacGraw are literally thrown away as they hide in a dump bin. It is also noteworthy that the cynical 70's allow the two good/bad guy leads to get away with it in the end. (A strange tacked-on note added only to the version for Spain

Ali does not like herself at all, she tells the
New York Times: "It wasn't my finest hour.
I'm sorry not to be better in it, but I'm not
about to break into tears."

before. The ironic truth is that McQueen is
actually at greater peace with himself than he
has been in years. The reason: the big romance
with Ali. To his astonishment he has found
another soul-mate who has replaced Neile in
his every thought. Marriage is again on his
mind, and he acts on it.

On July 12, 1973, Terence Stephen McQueen
marries Alice MacGraw Hoen Evans. His
second, her third. Months before, she'd told
Evans she was finished with him, and that
Grail-like *Gatsby* part has gone to the misera-
bly miscast Mia Farrow. Ali couldn't care less:
she's got what she wanted. McQueen's kids
attend the ceremony, which is held under the
cottonwoods on the shores of Lake Minnehaha
in Cheyenne, Wyoming, which McQueen
considers the last unspoiled United State. She
wears a beige knit blouse and pastel plaid
miniskirt to his levis. It is a standard ceremony, with no personalized vows or pre-nuptial
agreements. Just the old "I do."

Thus said, McQueen begins the hunt for
another vehicle to star them together.

informs audiences that "Doc" and "Carol" were
apprehended six weeks later. The last frame of
the Spanish special edition shows McQueen re-
entering jail, in a concession to the Fascist
regime's censors.)

Despite good notices from Judith Crist in
New York and Stanley Kaufmann in *New
Republic*, the movie is brutally panned. Harvard *Lampoon* places it high on its annual "Ten
Worst" list, and gives the Natalie Wood Worst
Actress Award to Ali, while Peckinpah receives
the Wrong-Way Corrigan Memorial Flight
Jacket for Bad Direction. Nevertheless, audiences flock to see the movie, to the tune of $35
million, far greater than even Boasberg's
original optimistic prediction.

Critics and audiences alike particularly note
that McQueen has never allowed the fiery side
of his nature to come out so boldly on screen

Rona Barrett can smell the breakup coming when she
hears Ali is dancing bare-breasted with indie producer
Larry Spengler at Studio 54, and when McQueen signs
Linda Evans for *Tom Horn*.

McQueen is author Henri Charriere's personal choice to play the autobiographical role.

Papillon

ALLIED ARTISTS, 1973

CREDITS

Director, *Franklin J. Schaffner;* producers, *Robert Dorfmann, Schaffner;* executive producer, *Ted Richmond;* associate producer, *Robert Laffont;* screenplay, *Dalton Trumbo, Lorenzo Semple, Jr.,* from the book by *Henri Charriere;* photographer, *Fred Koenekamp* (Technicolor, Panavision); editor, *Robert Swink;* production design, *Anthony Masters;* music, *Jerry Goldsmith;* costumes, *Anthony Powell;* casting, *Jack Baur.*

CAST

Papillon *(STEVE McQUEEN),* Louis Dega *(Dustin Hoffman),* Indian Chief *(Victor Jory),* Julot *(Don Gordon),* Leper Colony Chief *(Anthony Zerbe),* Maturette *(Robert Deman),* Clusiot *(Woodrow Parfrey),* Lariot *(Bill Mumy),* Dr. Chatal *(George Coulouris),* Zoraima *(Ratna Assan),* Commandant *(Dalton Trumbo),* Sergeant *(Vic Tayback).*

LOCATIONS: Spain, Jamaica.
A Corona/General Production Company Production.
MPAA rating: PG (appealed from original R).
Opened December 16, 1973 (150 minutes).

REVIEWS

"A big, brave, stouthearted, sometimes romantic, sometimes silly melodrama. As played by McQueen, Papillon is as all-American as a Rover Boy" (Vincent Canby, *New York Times*).
"A monument to the eternal desire of moviemakers to impress people and win awards. To put McQueen in a role that requires intense audience identification with the hero's humanity is madness. McQueen is an amazing actor of considerable skill, but a reserved actor whose expressive resources are very small. If ever there was a wrong actor for a man of great spirit, it's McQueen" (Pauline Kael, *The New Yorker*).
"The atmosphere bored into the brain like it does to its victims, leaving them as well as an audience stunned, disoriented, incredulous, and nearly catatonic. It takes literally hours to come out of 'Papillon' " *(Variety).*

Though *The Getaway* has accomplished some kind of setback in image, McQueen's

200

visibility is strong enough to land him his most financially rewarding role yet. It is the title part as *Papillon*, from Henri Charriere's international best-seller.

The book was a romanticized version of one man's quest for freedom, a memoir of Charriere's decades of imprisonment for the murder of a pimp, particularly detailing the effects of isolation and spiritual debasement at the hands of French authorities who incarcerated the little Frenchman on dreaded Devil's Island, off the coast of Venezuela. His courage in the face of overwhelming emotional desolation was the substance of the book, which sold five million copies in America and 17 million abroad. And he is more than happy to make it into a movie, as long as someone is willing to give him $550,000 and a percentage. Already Roman Polanski has discussed such a film, which would star Warren Beatty, but lack of financing has ended talks.

Numerous Devil's Island movies had been made over the years. Bogart was there in the *Casablanca* follow-up *Passage to Marseilles.* Gable got out of it in *Strange Cargo.* Karloff haunted *Devil's Island.* And Jim Brown was the "I" in *I Escaped from Devil's Island.*

And every variation on the prison movie has been done to this point: glossy studio version *(20,000 Years in Sing Sing)*, blaxploitation *(Riot)*, work farm *(Cool Hand Luke)*, women behind bars *(Caged)*, teenage crime *(Riot in Juvenile Prison)*, the social reform film *(I Was a Fugitive from a Chain Gang)*, the strict

THE GREATEST ADVENTURE OF ESCAPE!

STEVE McQUEEN DUSTIN HOFFMAN

in a FRANKLIN J. SCHAFFNER film

PAPILLON

PANAVISION° TECHNICOLOR° **PG**

TWO MEN
WITH NOTHING IN COMMON
BUT A WILL TO LIVE
AND A PLACE TO DIE.

Allied Artists tries very hard to give the public the impression that *Papillon* is another *Great Escape*-type film for McQueen fans. (All pictures copyright © 1973 by Allied Artists Pictures Corporation)

201

Charriére is present on the Jamaican shoot, but he dies July 29, 1973, of lung cancer, without seeing the epic film he has inspired. The film's premiere benefits cancer research, in his memory.

actioner *(Riot in Cell Block Nine)*, the homo-sexual exposé *(Fortune and Men's Eyes)*, and the best of them all, *Brute Force*. The variations go on and on: *The Great Escape* and *The McKenzie Break* doing similar chores for POW's; the musical version, *Jailhouse Rock;* the fast-buck star vehicle, Charles Bronson in *Breakout;* the andante amidst the forte allegro, *Birdman of Alcatraz;* convict comedy, *We're No Angels.*

Every variation except one: spectacle. With that addition, some $12 million worth, *Papillon* intends to outdo them all, paradoxically setting one solitary man's struggle in the middle of huge production values.

For the one man, producers Robert Dorfmann and Franklin Schaffner secure Steve McQueen at the record-breaking fee of $2 million. Dustin Hoffman, a strong marquee name in his own right, is signed as support for $1¼ million. Schaffner will direct for the comparatively minimal $750,000. Before the cameras are even loaded with the Technicolor stock, $4 million, a third of the film's budget, has been spent on the major above-the-line salaries alone. (Once blacklisted screenwriter Dalton Trumbo makes pittance, but gets to

202

Co-star Dustin Hoffman had to wear special contact lenses to balance his vision, severely distorted by the Coke-bottle spectacles he used as part of his characterization. His former wife Ann makes an unbilled cameo appearance as the wife he embraces before embarking for prison.

The tremors of anticipation of seeing how Hoffman would work subordinate to McQueen's role are abated when the men behave absolutely professionally on the set, speaking not a word to each other between the takes or after principal photography is completed.

play the commandant who addresses the prisoners before they sail, a scene shot with a thousand extras.)

The McQueen/Hoffman/Schaffner triumvirate is worth it. Allied Artists is scraping every cent together to make sure it has a nice big expensive smash. This delicious irony is not lost on McQueen: the studio where McQueen made his supporting-role debut in *Never Love a Stranger* just 15 years before now hands him a paycheck greater than the sum of his first four films' entire shooting budgets combined. And he is starred over First Artists partner Hoffman, who can easily carry a film on his own. McQueen highly approves of Schaffner, a Phi Beta Kappa who has lately found himself on the A list with Oscars for *Patton* and kudos for *Nicholas and Alexandra.* He is the director to get when you want something enormous put on screen.

Together, the three men ensure Allied Artists a good return on its investment, which it cannot afford to lose. The investment is secured by declaring the film an official French production, for corporate tax reasons.

Besides the generous fee, McQueen is given an artistic freedom he has never had before,

Director Franklin Schaffner (in the hat) and director of photography Fred Koenekamp on location in Jamaica.

203

since the film will be shot largely in sequence, rare for a film of such scope. This will allow him to build his character in stages, as his theatrical training has taught him, unlike motion pictures which are constructed like a jigsaw puzzle.

He sets up housekeeping on Jamaica for the duration, commuting back and forth across the island for each day's work. Studio interiors are shot in Montego Bay, and the prison set is built in Falmouth, 20 miles east on the north shore of the island. The prison set is the largest in the film, an 800-foot-long expanse, the product of two years of research by production designer Anthony Masters. On the other side, at Ocho Rios, the Devil's Island and Indian village sequences are staged. In Kingston, the crew films the arrival of the prison ship in the screenplay's setting of French Guyana. And in Savanah-la-Mar, the Paradise Jungle Park doubles for work camp settings. The company has taken over Jamaica.

Papillon is cemented as a Christmas package for 1973, opening to advance distribution deals guaranteeing the film at least $7 million. Ultimately it will garner a $20 million domestic gross, due largely to the unusually steep $2 million AA spends on promotion. Little is released about the film during its making; then

On Jamaica, Hindu Indians substitute for the book's Guajiri Indians.

204

Unusual publicity ploys include a three-page topless spread in *Playboy* on actress Ratna Assan, the only woman of note in the film.

the studio unloads it with maximum saturation. The tactics, contrary to all previous roadshow presentations, work: four weeks into the run, the film has made $11.3 million.

In its first application to the MPAA, the film has received a largely deserved R rating, allowing no one in the theater below the age of 16, 17, 18, or 21, depending on the whim of the governing community, without accompanying parent. Allied Artists and the producers appeal the rating, which is subsequently changed to a PG—parental guidance suggested. The MPAA faces its first legal test of the rating system when an Illinois father, who has taken his children to see the movie, sues over the PG tag. But a Chicago Federal Court throws the $7¼ million lawsuit out of court, ignoring the opening shot of a hundred naked men, the heavily ladled violence and profanity, and the extended scenes of bare-breasted Indian women, whom the MPAA apparently finds less sexually explicit than similar scenes with white women would have been. The judge declares that the rating is a warning and that the father has acted despite the rating. But the successful

Mostly McQueen looks terrible in the movie. Early on he's all right, but after years in solitary, this is what he looks like.

The huge prison camp set on a slow day. A colony of expatriate Germans living on Jamaica is enlisted to populate the camp set for crowd scenes.

MPAA appeal and ensuing legal reinforcement are early indicators that a studio can pretty much get any rating it wants, if a lot of money is resting on the picture.

But that isn't the end of *Papillon*'s court sessions. A dispute over TV rights erupts in September, 1974, when CBS announces it has received broadcast rights, immediately answered by ABC's claim it has bought TV privileges from Allied Artists for $3¾ million. The argument becomes the best-known conflict of the day between studios and producers regarding ownership of network licensing rights. The dispute is a result of independent negotiations, those of producers Dorfmann and Ted Richmond with CBS, and of AA with ABC. Supposedly, the film cannot be shown on TV before December, 1978, according to a five-year clause in the original contracts, but it ends up on CBS in October, 1977. So much for contracts.

Then Hoffman sues for his full percentage payments, which he says he has not received. The suit vanishes when AA goes belly up in 1980, with Lorimar acquiring Allied Artists' entire film library, which it has had to sell to pay its bankruptcy debts. The package, worth $7 million, includes *Cabaret, The Betsy*, and *Papillon*.

All this accumulated angst is absurd after seeing *Papillon*, which is a financial exercise rather than an artistic one. Its merits are quantitative, not qualitative. Yes, it shows every penny of its budget, but it is a bore. Its honest location filming is an enormous aid, as is the lab process that drains the color and washes each shot in a dusty amber. But it has that Big Movie attitude that a costly pre-sold mega-hit must be slow and ponderous to give the public every cent of its inflated hard-ticket admission price. Time is money. It seems to duplicate in screen time and real time the experience of the lingering existential death it takes to survive in prison. Schaffner is intent on the audience's experiencing Devil's Island, not merely visiting it.

The film has all the clichés of the prison film, but endows them with a new ugliness overlying the cliché to make it something new. Papillon in solitary is just a more grizzled version of Hilts the Cooler King in *The Great Escape*, subtracting a catcher's mitt and adding insects to make you squirm as you pity.

The disgusting is italicized: a prisoner's decapitated head splashes blood on the camera lens, a rifle wound pumps blood arterially, a centipede is sectioned with a spoon edge and dumped into a vomitous soup in solitary, a cut throat dribbles on beach sand, bug-gnawed corpses populate jungle underbrush, an escapee is impaled on a spring-driven punjab stick, and sad, rotting lepers hide in huts and scarify with makeup heavy on horror and empty of pathos. Overall, a depressing collection of details Schaffner and screenwriter Dalton Trumbo find necessary to liven things up.

Oddest of all is McQueen himself, deeply tanned, deeply lined, sun-bleached hair cut tight to the scalp. He plays the character with pure American accent, pushing pieces of his real self through the character: a ballsy defiance asserted without regard for consequence but which must be declared out of basic human integrity, and a surprising humor in the midst of stress, delivered with an incongruous blue-eyed twinkle.

He gets royal treatment in a real star part. He has comparatively little dialogue: most of his acting is via his makeup, which gives him several guises through the movie: the nut-brown man who first comes to the prison camp, the dapper period dresser of an ineptly directed dream sequence, the silence-maddened white rat, the mustachioed escapee, the lean beachcomber at peace, the crippled silver-haired Devil's Island inhabitant whose five years in solitary age him 20.

McQueen earns his money, doing a physically miserable film. He's chained arm to leg behind his back on a tabletop, forced to eat like a dog out of a tin plate; he drags logs through a filthy gray tropical swamp and shares his area with a live and feisty crocodile (no doubling for McQueen here); and he is ragged and stubbly throughout most of the picture.

But the bottom line on the casting is this: McQueen is wrong for the part, regardless of Charriere's preference. The Academy recognizes this shattering fault, despite AA's publicizing McQueen's Oscar case as a long overdue nod of appreciation and acknowledgement. The only nomination the picture receives is for Best Original Dramatic Score, which it loses to Marvin Hamlisch's music for *The Way We Were*. McQueen doesn't even make it into the semis. He has tried. He has done all the right things: big part, big salary, big picture, big director, big opportunity. But he is still the wrong man for the role.

That's it, that's all, and that's that.

Papillon makes his bid for freedom.

The Towering Inferno

20TH CENTURY-FOX/WARNER BROTHERS, 1974

CREDITS

Dialogue director, *John Guillermin;* producer, action director, *Irwin Allen;* associate producer, *Sidney Marshall;* photographer, *Fred Koenekamp* (DeLuxe Color, Panavision, Stereophonic Sound); editors, *Harold F. Kress, Carl Kress;* production designer, *William Creber;* music, *John Williams;* casting, *Jack Baur;* costumes, *Paul Zastupnevich;* special photographic effects, *L.B. Abbott;* stunt coordinator, *Paul Stader;* mechanical effects, *A.D. Flowers, Logan Frazee.*

CAST

Michael O'Hallorhan *(STEVE McQUEEN),* Doug Roberts *(Paul Newman),* Susan Franklin *(Faye Dunaway),* James Duncan *(William Holden),* Harlee Claiborne *(Fred Astaire),* Patty Simmons *(Susan Blakely),* Roger Simmons *(Richard Chamberlain),* Lisolette Mueller *(Jennifer Jones),* Jernigan *(O.J. Simpson),* Sen. Gary Parker *(Robert Vaughn),* Dan Bigelow *(Robert Wagner),* Lorrie *(Susan Flannery),* Kappy *(Don Gordon),* Paula Ramsay *(Sheila Mathews),* Singer *(Maureen McGovern).*

Original ad art staggers McQueen's and Newman's names so that each appears to have top billing. That isn't the case in reality. (All pictures copyright © 1974 by 20th Century-Fox Film Corporation)

LOCATIONS: San Francisco.
MPAA rating: PG.
Opened December 18, 1974 (165 minutes).

REVIEWS

"A suspense film for arsonists, firemen, movie-technology buffs, building inspectors, worry warts. It appears to have been less directed than physically constructed. Overwrought and silly in its personal drama, but the visual spectacle is first-rate. A vivid, completely safe nightmare" (Vincent Canby, *New York Times*). "The arrival of Steve McQueen as the Fire Chief signals that the action proper has begun. It all boils down to the moment when Newman and McQueen face each other over a packet of plastic explosive. Monolithic casting" (Russell Davies, *The Observer*).

From the awesome, expensive bore that was *Papillon*, McQueen enters contractual negotiations for his appearance in what will be the biggest picture of 1974, Irwin Allen's $15 million production of *The Towering Inferno*.

It is the year's most splendid disaster movie. The cycle of movie disasters—natural, not critical—has begun with Allen's 1972 film *The Poseidon Adventure*, quite an achievement in putting a bushel of Oscar winners together in a confined situation and watching them fight their way out of it. Hearkening back to predecessors *The Bridge of San Luis Rey* (1944) and *The High and the Mighty* (1954), the new film will again focus on a number of stars in a life-or-death situation.

The film is born of two books. There's one novel, *The Tower*, which takes its impetus from a 1970 skyscraper fire at One New York Plaza. Bids for the film rights start at $200,000 and go to $390,000 before everyone else lets Warner Brothers have it. Eight weeks later, Allen finds a similar novel, *The Glass Inferno*, bids for it, and buys it for Fox at $400,000.

But everyone remembers how the two Harlow pictures knocked each other out of the skies back in '65, and in this nervous New Hollywood, no one wants to take a chance. So Gordon Stulberg of Fox calls up Ted Ashley of Warners, and after a few arcane negotiations, these two wizards of odds agree to co-finance a single picture that will combine certain elements of each book in equal proportion.

Stirling Silliphant sets about the laborious writing and re-writing task, fusing plots, characters, and situations. He figures out a means of taking seven figures from each book, and extracts each novel's set-piece climax: from one, the lifeline rescue to a neighboring rooftop, and from the other, the spectacular dynamiting of the water tanks.

While Silliphant interlaces, the studios divide, each company putting up half the budget in return for domestic receipts for Fox and foreign gross for Warners. It is the first time two majors have combined resources to produce a single picture. *Poseidon*'s $160 million worldwide box-office take is a constant reassurance.

Working closely with both studios' brass, especially at Fox where he has been a producer for years, Irwin Allen puts the film on 2600 storyboards, scene by scene, so that everyone will know what he and they are doing. He and director John Guillermin, a craftsmanlike Britisher with no personal style whatsoever, work carefully with Silliphant, devising a plan by which the film can be made as two simultaneous productions, one dialogue and one action. A gaffer on one half can't do the work on the other half, so widely separated in technique and execution are the two jobs.

The soldered novels make up the manufactured movie title *The Towering Inferno*, which is officially announced January, 1974. It immediately arouses the ire of the construction and real estate industries, most particularly in New York, where the controversial twin towers of the World Trade Center are being completed 110 stories over the harbor. New York fire commissioner James T. O'Hagan is quick to deny the probability of such a disaster as the

and the dazzling Hyatt Regency indoor glass elevators are spliced next to 110-foot-tall mockups of the skyscraper to blend into a cohesive whole.

Back in the Los Angeles area, the basement of a Century City office building duplicates script requirements for an elaborate computer-controlled building surveillance and maintenance center. Set decorations are smart and classy, capped by $1.5 million in paintings, including four Picassos, loaned to Allen by millionaire art collector Norton Simon, husband of one of the stars, Jennifer Jones, and himself a major Fox stockholder.

The promenade deck on the top floor of the 135-story edifice is the single largest set of the picture, 11,000 square feet of teak and azure dining elegance, just right for the soon-to-be-trapped VIP's. A 340-foot twinkling San Francisco skyline cyclorama completes the $300,000 set, which will be entirely gutted for the watery finale. That conclusion involves the unleashing of the rooftop water tanks, which hold a million gallons (though purists argue

film will portray, but he still admits queasiness over the possibility: "I'd sleep a lot better at night if the World Trade Center had sprinklers," he tells the *New York Times.* Allen underlines the statement, adding that there is no fire-fighting equipment anywhere in the world that can extinguish a blaze above a seventh floor.

Critical and consumer camps are thus divided between those who see the film as a warning and those who condemn it, even before it's made, as glossy sensationalism. As the debates continue, the picture picks up unbuyable publicity. The attention it is getting is international: a spokesman for the medical industry in Scotland declares the film will be required viewing in all Scottish hospitals.

Meanwhile in California, grand sets arise. For the skyscraper interiors, five floors are constructed at Fox's Malibu ranch for close-up work. High-rises in San Francisco double for the plaza and lobby scenes during the crew's three weeks of location shooting in July, 1974. Pieces of the Bank of America's plaza entrance

Veteran producer Irwin Allen takes charge of directing the action half of the picture, leaving dialogue direction to John Guillermin.

McQueen, Dunaway, and Newman share a between-scenes joke while on location in San Francisco.

One reason for the lack of friction between the two headliners is the perfect balance of their parts, two men cooperating as two halves of a solution to a problem whose urgency is immediate.

Most suspenseful moment in the picture: an outdoor elevator dangles from a cable lowered by helicopter, as McQueen clings to its roof trying desperately to hold on to a helpless fireman (Ernie Orsatti) a thousand feet above the ground. A real white-knuckle moment!

Allen originally wants McQueen for what turns out to be Newman's role as the architect of the burning building, but McQueen argues for and wins the part of the tough fire chief.

Rescue chopper and a breeches buoy save VIP's trapped by
flames. The helicopter is real; the flaming skyscraper is a
1/14th scale "miniature" as tall as a 10-story building in its
own right.

Disaster strikes the breeches buoy. Audiences always cheer when bad guy Chamberlain, a contractor whose inferior materials have caused the conflagration, tumbles to his smashing death. Yay!

25 have been hired just to "die." Some of the individual stunts are so dangerous that the performers receive $1000 a day, as opposed to the standard $172. Most of the stunts involve people who have to look as if they are aflame. They are doused with alcohol and benzine, then ignited. To remain safe, they wear three sets of special underwear designed originally to protect drivers in the Indianapolis 500, and are further outfitted with hidden compressed-air breathing devices, under fake facial and hand skin and false hair. In the most complicated pieces of action, burning stunters are blown back by explosions through breakaway movie glass. Safety precautions are enforced. There are just two tiny injuries, one stuntwoman who is singed around the mouth, and a man who receives a cut over his eye from a piece of

that no such tank currently holds more than 25,000 gallons). Seven Panavision and five videotape cameras are positioned so as not to miss a drop of the deluge, which drains into a pit below the set built on stilts 25 feet above the ground.

At the peak of production, four camera crews are shooting on any of some 57 sets on one Fox back lot, a record. The sets are packed with stars and extras, as well as 60 stuntpeople, who do 200 stunts for the picture. Of the 60,

214

A stuntwoman impersonating Jennifer Jones falls out of a crippled outside elevator.

falling plaster as he walks off the set following a wrap. Small wonder that requests to visit the sets exceed those for any other film now in production. Everybody especially wants to see the final holocaust that leaves only eight of the original 57 sets standing.

The stuntpeople may be the true stars of the picture, but their names aren't on the marquee. In fact, there isn't enough room on any marquee to list the top-liners, cannily chosen as somebody for everyone.

Daytime TV watchers get their first wide-screen look at Susan Flannery of *Days of Our Lives* (though she quits the soap opera soon after the movie comes out). Robert Wagner comes in for a brief nod in the matinee-idol direction. Robert Vaughn, who has just played Harry Truman for TV, takes the familiar role of a political figure in this, his third movie with McQueen. Blacks receive representation in the form of former Buffalo Bills football star O. J. Simpson. Sentimentalists revel in the teaming of Fred Astaire and Jennifer Jones to show love exists for the over-50 set. Richard Chamberlain catches an against-type villain's role, but still appeals to baby boomers who have grown up on *Dr. Kildare.* William Holden is back in the public eye after winning an Emmy for his *Blue Knight* miniseries, and brings nostalgia in the door with his personage. Model Susan Blakeley is a pretty face trying to prove herself an actress. Real acting is handled by Faye Dunaway, who doesn't have a single moment with McQueen, despite their previous *Thomas Crown.* Surrounding them are 2800 extras.

And at the top of the list are Steve McQueen and Paul Newman.

In that order.

See, Steve McQueen is a very, very big star. So big that fan Kent Twitchell, an advanced art student at Cal State at Los Angeles, expresses his fandom by painting an enormous portrait of McQueen all over the side of a two-story building at 1151 S. Union Street in L.A. It makes papers all over the country, and *Oui* magazine, too. Tributes like this can go to a guy's head, dig?

So McQueen makes his terms to Irwin Allen simple and mean: he and Paul Newman are each to receive $1 million flat, plus 7½ percent of the producer's gross. And McQueen is to receive top billing in the picture, over Paul Newman. Irwin Allen agrees.

Authoress Erica Jong *(Fear of Flying)* on the subject of McQueen in *Esquire:* "Who has the bluest eyes? Newman or McQueen? It's difficult to say, but McQueen's twinkle more. He makes me think of all those leathery-necked cowboys at remote truck stops in Nevada. Does he wear pointy boots? And does he take them off when he screws?"

His terms to screenwriter Silliphant are equally terse: he wants exactly the same number of lines as Newman, no more, no less, definitely not less. Silliphant tells *Women's Wear Daily* that "Steve has a nagging instinct of what is right for him based on his ability. He doesn't like long speeches. He likes them to be terse, sharp, almost proverbial." What Silliphant doesn't say is what a pain in the ass he thinks McQueen is.

Steve has a special gym built on the lot so he can continue his karate lessons between shooting sessions. He and Dunaway are the only stars who leave strict orders not to be approached by visitors to the set. McQueen goes one step further, unconditionally refusing to grant any interviews to any press. Newman, however, merely requests that he not be surprised.

Both McQueen and Newman have to do many of their own stunts because the close-in design of the camerawork will instantly reveal doubling. More free publicity showers down as McQueen is on stage 5 at Samuel Goldwyn Studios, working on his role with LA Fire

215

'Towering Inferno' Plays for Real in L.A.

The picture's smash status is aided by such coverage as this real-life parallels no press agent could hope to invent.

Department Battalion Chief Peter Lucarelli. Suddenly an alarm on another sound stage calls the chief to the scene. There, during the taping of the children's show *Sigmund*, an electrical fire has broken out and McQueen goes along with Lucarelli for some real on-the-job training. Wirephotos of a sweaty fireman Steve McQueen make all the nation's newspapers.

And how do these two megastars get along? Beautifully, is the crew consensus. Part of the secret lies in their mutual love for racing. Newman has been racing on and off for a decade, and has competed at Bonneville. His biking around Hollywood is exactly McQueen's style. The two men, cool yet friendly, show nary a sign of competitiveness on the sound stage, no hint of trying to steal scenes from one another. If there is room for correction in a scene, they freely suggest alternatives, since both their contracts give them personal approval of all shots.

The motion picture premieres with great hoopla at the Avco Theater in Westwood, California. It is a benefit for the Diabetes Association of Southern California, so arranged because Fox president Stulberg is diabetic. Stars and celebrities, minus McQueen, attend a post-premiere party at the Beverly Hilton, under the sponsorship of Mary Tyler Moore and Jack Benny, to benefit the American Diabetes Association. Some $84,700 is raised at the glamorous event. It is paralleled on the East Coast by Fox chairman of the board Dennis Stanfill's 500-person party at the Four Seasons. There, in honor of the movie, a five-foot-tall cake is set aflame.

The Towering Inferno opens just before Christmas to rave reviews for the technical effects and qualified kudos for the rest of the package. Audiences, however, crowd into soldout screenings so they can see what people look like when they burn. And they see it with crystal clarity thanks to Peter Myers, domestic distribution vice-president for Fox. He sets a new standard for projection: for 500-plus capacity houses, he requires a 100-watt amplifier system with A-4 speakers and 16 foot-candle illumination.

With the opening, the picture starts raking in cash as few pictures have in recent memory. Thanks to the Nixon recession, people are again turning to movies as their escape, and are pouring dollars into box offices with the most eagerness since record year 1946. Every big picture released during 1974 and 1975 is a new box-office record-breaker, and *Inferno* is destined to be the champion until the phenomenal *Jaws* surpasses it six months later. Eventually, domestic and foreign receipts will pass the magic $100 million mark, ensuring the film a permanent, if sooty, niche in Hollywood's financial pantheon.

Along with the money come the honors. The Academy nominations total eight, three behind the top-nominated *Chinatown* and *Godfather II*, to which it loses Best Picture, Best Supporting Actor (Robert De Niro over sentimental favorite Fred Astaire), Best Score, and Best Art Direction. The Sound award goes to *Earthquake*'s Sensurround. But *Inferno* does capture the cinematography, editing, and original song awards, and the "Winner of Three Academy Awards!" sign goes up in the window.

The movie's fiery warnings hit home to its immediate family. Taking his own advice, Irwin Allen moves his Pierre Hotel suite in New York from the 38th floor to the fifth, and Paul Newman stops going to his 14th-floor dentist. Yet there is still that moral quandary, where one must balance the picture's dedication to the firefighters of America against the vicarious thrills of watching people die. Half the movie is genuine warning, half is cheap thrills. The crafty Allen has played both ends against the middle and won.

What the film has meant personally for both McQueen and Newman is that it has given them a chance to act together. It's a treat that occasions many a theatergoer (personally witnessed) to say, "Isn't this something, seeing both of them together?"

But the millions of dollars McQueen has made off the movie is still not the biggest thing about it, nor the most important. Seeing Newman and McQueen on screen simultaneously at last answers the question that has ached in the hearts of the innumerable for half the fifties, all the sixties, and half the seventies. In 18 years, McQueen has risen from an unbilled bit player in a Newman starrer to billing over Newman as the top name in the biggest picture of the year, a blinding nova of the first magnitude that now and for all time gives The Answer to the minions:

Steve McQueen's eyes are bluer.

An Enemy of the People

WARNER BROTHERS, 1978

Central to McQueen's convictions about the necessity of courage is the character of Dr. Thomas Stockmann, who is alone in his ethical battle to warn his hometown about pollutants in the healing springs that have made the town famous. (All pictures copyright © 1978 by Warner Brothers, Inc.)

CREDITS

Producer-director, *George Schaefer;* executive producer, *STEVE McQUEEN;* associate producer, *Philip Parslow;* screenplay, *Alexander Jacobs,* from the *Arthur Miller* translation of the *Henrik Ibsen* play; photographer, *Paul Lohmann* (Technicolor, Panavision); editor, *Sheldon Kahn;* production design, *Eugene Lourie;* music, *Leonard Rosenman;* casting, *Mike Fenton, Jane Feinberg;* costumes, *Noel Taylor.*

CAST

Dr. Thomas Stockmann *(STEVE McQUEEN),* Peter Stockmann *(Charles Durning),* Catherine Stockmann *(Bibi Andersson),* Morton Kiil *(Eric Christmas),* Hovstad *(Michael Cristofer),* Aslaksen *(Richard A. Dysart).*

A Solar Production presented by First Artists.
MPAA rating: PG.
Opened March 17, 1978 (103 minutes).

REVIEWS

"Think of Clark Gable as the tragic 'Parnell,' or Gregory Peck playing Ahab as if he were Abraham Lincoln. Recall Elizabeth Taylor as the Cleopatra of Great Neck. Then add to this list of big-star follies the typically lean, tight-lipped action hero Steve McQueen. Here he's plump, bearded, and avuncular, a bit like old Kris Kringle. For McQueen to play Ibsen's volatile, idealistic intellectual Dr. Stockmann is as unusual as it would be for Dr. Carl Sagan to try and play Darth Vader" (Michael Sragow, *Los Angeles Herald-Examiner*).
"The problem has nothing to do with the abandonment of a successful action-adventure image, but rather the unsuitability of this particular actor to this particular role" (*Variety*).
"He lends a quiet dignity. Although lacking the voice and authority to sustain Ibsen's intense confrontation scenes, it is by no means a bad

performance. It nevertheless lacks the sweep and stature to make it a memorable one" (Arthur Knight, *Hollywood Reporter*).

Like *The Towering Inferno*, Steve McQueen's world now starts to burn down. While still five years away from the final consuming blaze, the match has been lit, and there's already some smoke in the basement. He knows nothing of it yet.

It is a leisurely year: 1975. Steve is so rich from his films he doesn't have to work, so he throws himself into his marriage to Ali, and lets it be known he is available only in tandem with her. Nobody is interested, and it gets a little stormy. Ali is seen lunching chummily with ex-husband Robert Evans, freshly estranged from his latest wife, Phyllis George. Steve is seen roaring around Beverly Hills with a new bike and a new beard. Their private fights become public knowledge. There is even a marvelous rumor afloat that says Steve, pining for ex-wife Neile, has invited her to live with the two of them in a *ménage a trois* on his Trancas property north of Malibu. Ali starts up psychoanalysis five times a week, and Steve starts reassessing their relationship.

Then, quickly, the storm passes, and a significant icon passes between them. Steve has a $2,000 pair of erotically engraved belt buckles made as a peace offering. The implication is startling: the buckles depict Adam offering Eve the apple. The point of splitting is possibly past. They buy a new house in Palm Springs, and Ali decorates it herself, tossing in $4,000 worth of wicker in one throw. When they're not in Palm Springs or Trancas, they can be found soaking up the serenity somewhere in the 1,000 acres of Ventana, Big Sur's chic spa.

There are still the movies to think about, though, and Steve wants to get back into them. Unable to find a director interested in working with the two of them—that bothersome lack of chemistry in *The Getaway* is why—McQueen announces in the fall that he will co-star with Ali in his directorial debut, the project an as-yet untitled comedy Western for which he is having a script personally tailored. He turns down Elliott Kastner, who has approached them to star in his *Deajum's Wife*, because the offer has come after Steve has decided to become a director himself. *Deajum's Wife* is never made.

Nothing is coming off. He has a chance to do his first Western in years, *The Johnson County War* for director Michael Winner, a super action director with whom he might be willing to work if the price is right. But budget problems hit the film. McQueen sees there isn't going to be his kind of money in it, and heads for the exit. The movie goes to another director, Michael Cimino, who reworks the material and retitles it *Heaven's Gate*. A plan to star them together with Laurence Olivier in *The Betsy* is unfulfilled, and the parts go to Robert Duvall and Katherine Ross. Ali is growing restless, and Steve is already becoming bored. So bored he takes a $175 per week job doing bike stunts in a drive-in flick called *Dixie Dynamite*. He does so without taking screen billing. Ali lets it be known she'd like nothing better than to take the role of Isadora Wing in Julia Phillips' adaptation of Erica Jong's *Fear of Flying*, more than any part she's ever wanted. Steve says no. She is offered the female lead opposite Warren Beatty in his proposed remake of *Here Comes Mr. Jordan*. Steve says no. The part goes to Julie Christie and the picture becomes *Heaven Can Wait*. Ali is not pleased.

Neither is Steve. He stops doing his daily two-hour workout for the first time since Chino, and without the sit-ups the beer goes right to his ever-increasing belly. Thirty pounds of it. His hair, once short and straight, now kinks its way down to his shoulders. He sprouts an uncharacteristic shaggy beard that ages him a decade. He lets himself go so much that Paul Newman does not recognize him at a party.

Steve McQueen appears hell-bent on destroying the image that has made him rich. Part of the cause is that old male bugaboo, mid-life crisis, and part of it is his insistence on turning his back on the Hollywood he hates so much. He has always been far removed from that ilk in his dynamic spirit, and now he shows his contempt by changing his physical appearance from trim to slovenly. His rebel nature takes literal form in the way he looks.

He no longer pays lip service to the people who have put him where he is. Joe Levine, producer of *Nevada Smith*, is building *A Bridge Too Far*, and makes his old friend an offer. But Steve wants three million to do the movie, plus he wants Levine to buy his $470,000 Palm Springs home, and also to put

Bursting with boredom, McQueen takes a stuntman's job on this low-budget bike comedy.

a buddy on the payroll for fifty grand. Joe says no. Steve is blasé.

He is offered a tremendous part, that of Willard in Francis Ford Coppola's update of Joseph Conrad's *Heart of Darkness,* the film that will go through a torture chamber before it becomes *Apocalypse Now.* Coppola calls it "the most violent film ever," and McQueen proves it by demanding $1.5 million for 16 weeks' work in the Philippines. Then he decides he wants another $1.5 million deferred. And then he doesn't want to work 16 weeks, he wants to work three, and he doesn't want the part of Willard, he wants to play Kurtz, for which Marlon Brando is about to be signed. Coppola shows him the door, replaces him with Harvey Keitel, who is fired and replaced by Martin Sheen, who has a heart attack. On the basis of losing McQueen, Coppola has to return $5 million of the $21 million his European distributors have given him on the strength of having signed McQueen in the first place. Then he ends up giving Brando the $3 million salary McQueen demanded, the $3 million Coppola has previously said he would never give any actor for any part in any movie at any time.

McQueen thinks it's just as well. But still he is bored.

His ennui abates momentarily because there is a madman in Africa named Idi Amin Dada, who has taken a bunch of hostages at the Entebbe Airport in Uganda. Within hours of

Charles Durning is bombastically, magnificently cast as the town's mayor, in bitter opposition to Stockmann.

220

The good doctor preaches his right to speak the truth to an almost convinced mayor.

the dramatic Israeli raid on the facility, which occurs during the early hours of America's Bicentennial celebration, every Hollywood heavy has gotten in on the action, and someone wants McQueen in on it, too.

Admittedly, the raid on Entebbe is the most spectacular commando event of the seventies. Nevertheless, there is an element of overkill in the number of separate projects that are announced.

Universal has the first entry in the sweepstakes, presenting a project to be directed by George Roy Hill. Paramount proposes a film to be adapted by Paddy Chayefsky from the Bantam paperback quickie *90 Minutes at Entebbe*, and Sidney Lumet is said to want to direct. But Warner Brothers has the best hand, announcing a $12 million movie with Franklin Schaffner directing and Steve McQueen starring, as Col. Dan Shomron, leader of the raid. Not only that: Warners chairman Ted Ashley has enlisted the whole-hearted support of the Israeli government in the making of the movie, an assistance which will be denied to all other comers. What is not said at this point is that Warners is very anxious to have McQueen star because it partially, but significantly, fulfills a contract of his dating back to 1968.

But there are problems. TV gets there much faster. Just 161 days after the raid, ABC has its own version on the air, a slapjack piece called *Victory at Entebbe*, with Richard Dreyfuss as Shomron. NBC gets its variation on four weeks

For his trouble, Stockmann is rewarded with persecution, stoning, and public censure.

221

The play ends with the statement, "The strong must learn to be lonely." It applies to McQueen's own life, more than ever.

later, *Raid on Entebbe*, with Charles Bronson as Shomron. And Israel is even planning its own movie, *Operation Thunderbolt*. There are simply too many players in the game, and Universal and Paramount drop out. Only Warners is left, and it saves face by claiming it is scrapping its intended project because it does not wish to compromise Israeli security procedures by detailing heretofore secret plans of the raid. The truth is that Warners has dropped out because there is too much competition and because McQueen has once more asked for too much money. He has priced himself out of a job again.

And McQueen has other things on his mind, anyway. Compulsively, he keeps collecting, and by 1977 he has amassed 53 cars, trucks, and bikes. He can race all he wants to without studio bosses sending memos to the set telling him he can't. But he has been looking in the mirror, and fat, unkempt, losing his youth at 46, he sees 50 coming around the corner a little too fast. He decides it's time to become an actor, and starts looking around for a project.

What better place to turn than the classics? That's all he did when he studied acting for six years, and it was the work that satisfied him the most. If he wants that kind of fulfillment again, he must return to the source.

He looks first at Russian author Nicolai Gogol's *The Inspector General*, made in 1949 as a comic vehicle for Danny Kaye. He wants to do it seriously, but his partner in the venture, director George Schaefer, thinks it's a bad idea. Schaefer's eight Emmys and four DGA awards make McQueen take note. Then he thinks about doing *Waiting for Godot*, but Samuel Beckett will not sell the screen rights to anyone. Finally, he reads, is entranced by, and buys Arthur Miller's American version of Henrik Ibsen's 1882 play *An Enemy of the People*. Schaefer warns him that others have walked this path before McQueen, without success. In 1974, Ely Landau had wanted to produce it for his American Film Theater series with Rod Steiger and Eva Marie Saint, but had given up on it when it proved unexciting as film fare. But McQueen think its ecologically oriented theme is timely, and its leading character, a bespectacled middle-aged doctor, precisely the kind of part he is looking for. He goes for it. It will be the first picture to carry his name in a capacity other than star: this one says frankly that he's executive producing, controlling it all the way.

And control it he does. First Artists reluctantly budgets the film at $2.5 million, incredibly low, but so intent on the production is

222

McQueen that he even foregoes his enormous asking price, just to convince First Artists, which he partly owns and runs, to make the damn thing. Warners will distribute, but they're only obliging to get McQueen going on his contractual obligation. He gets assistance which is disgruntled at best, but he is charging headlong into the film. He will not quit. He will not quit.

He should have quit.

Why, everybody wonders, is he so adamant about making a picture so blatantly wrong for him? According to James Bacon in the *Los Angeles Herald Examiner,* "Between his marriages to Ali MacGraw and Barbara Minty, McQueen had a beautiful black girl, a former Playboy bunny, as a girlfriend. She told me that McQueen intended to do *Enemy of the People* as a final rebellion to the Hollywood establishment, and then retire to life as a rancher." In other words, to do something personally rewarding without regard for the monetary consequences, because after the film it wouldn't matter to him anymore. Just one

movie as a classical actor: that's all he wants to do.

So the film has started out with the best and purest of intentions, but like most good intentions, it goes straight to hell with McQueen at the wheel.

The difficulties are apparent from the beginning. Schaefer is especially aware of them. "We're taking a long chance," he admits. "But if we can intrigue the McQueen fans and combine them with a more classical audience, the thing might work."

The thing doesn't work. This, despite his honest work. He assembles a watermark cast, importing from Sweden Ingmar Bergman's star Bibi Andersson (his first choice is Julie Harris, but she is unavailable—or uninterested). Nicol Williamson is set, but drops out, replaced by Charles Durning as McQueen's brother. Another casting coup is the signing of Michael Cristofer, a former actor lately known as the author of the play *The Shadow Box.*

McQueen handles everything. He demands strict adherence to the text past the point of

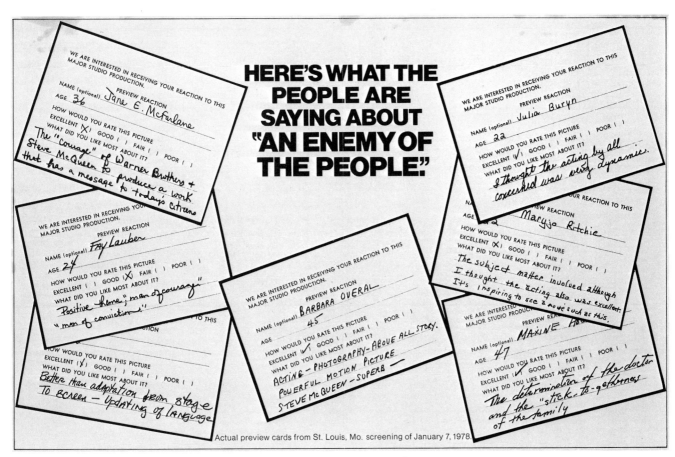

A curious but ineffective Warners ploy to make the film appeal to the mass audience.

223

fidelity into idolatry. He researches carefully, basing his character makeup on shots from a 1902 Scandinavian production. He thinks he is on the track of a hit when someone points out to him the script's oblique, disquieting, but perhaps seat-filling resemblance to *Jaws* (without the shark, naturally). He personally oversees the building of the lovely, authentic period sets on the MGM sound stages. And he forces himself to do a long speech at film's end, against his every instinct, and the effort nets him spontaneous applause on the set. He just knows he's doing everything right.

Warners is deeply troubled over the film. They have no idea how to market it. A year passes after the end of post-production and still they don't know what to do with it. Where are the people who could be nudged into seeing it, and why would they want to?

Finally, 18 months after the start of principal photography, Warners decides to test-market the film among the more literate college crowds, who are also big McQueen buffs. In March, 1978, with a general October release in mind, they aim a group sales pitch at colleges in Denver, Seattle, St. Louis, Santa Barbara, Minneapolis, and Tyler, Texas—not realizing everyone is gone for spring vacation. There just isn't anybody around to see the picture, and it is yanked in Minneapolis, for instance, after one week of a proposed four-week run, so dismal are the proceeds.

So they try new ads, surrounding the new bearded Ibsenized McQueen with shots of his previous roles, like *Bullitt* and *The Cincinnati Kid*, trying to prove to everyone that yes, folks, it really is Steve McQueen. This doesn't work either, and the studio has spent $400,000 just on make-aware campaigns.

Meanwhile, McQueen is putting everything he's got into promoting the picture. It is his function as executive producer to do so, he believes, and so he lines up an hour lecture on "The Genius of Ibsen" at UCLA. "McQueen doing Ibsen is like making a silk purse out of a sow's ear, let's face it," he tells the crowd. "At this point in my life, I don't want to make ordinary movies anymore. I spent a great deal of my life being a coward and spent a lot of time trying to overcome that influence. Ibsen showed the courage in the common man; that's why I did the film."

But the film dies. It is dead before it hits the screen. The public does not, will not want a simple story about a doctor who is alone in warning his hometown about severe water pollution, an imminent danger no one wants to admit to. Nobody wants to go to a movie about a major threat to a town's tourist industry unless that threat is, indeed, a shark.

The unthinkable happens. Unwilling to put another dime of promotion into the film, Warners pulls the picture from distribution and cancels its October release date.

McQueen is so distressed at the disastrous provincial reviews that he cancels his scheduled Oscar appearance, in which he was slated to award the Best Picture statuette.

In May, 1980, the studio offers the film as part of a 13-movie package available for purchase by pay-TV. The offers do not roll in, though Los Angeles' SelecTV picks it up for its August, 1980, schedule. The next year Warner Classics takes it over and releases it at last in New York at Joseph Papp's Public Theater, a home for orphan films. But even after its two-year hiatus from public sight, the film does not look that good.

The truth is brutal: the film's executive producer has chosen the wrong star for the lead. It is McQueen's first major failure, and despite his declaration that he didn't care what happened to the film as long as he got to do it, secretly he had expected it to be a smash. "I can afford to fail," he has exclaimed at the outset, but it has never dawned on him that he *could* fail. And he has failed, all right. No one has ever seen Steve McQueen crushed before. It is not a pretty sight.

Tom Horn

WARNER BROTHERS, 1980

CREDITS

Director, *William Wiard;* producer, *Fred Weintraub;* executive producer, *STEVE McQUEEN;* screenplay, *Thomas McGuane, Bud Shrake* from *Life of Tom Horn, Government Scout and Interpreter, Written by Himself;* photographer, *John Alonzo* (Technicolor, Panavision); editor, *George Grenville;* art director, *Ron Hobbs;* casting, *Sally Dennison;* costumes, *Luster Bayless;* stunt coordinator, *Gary Combs.*

CAST

Tom Horn *(STEVE McQUEEN),* Glendolene Kimmel *(Linda Evans),* John Coble *(Richard Farnsworth),* Joe Belle *(Billy Green Bush),* Sam Creedmore *(Slim Pickens),* Assistant Prosecutor *(Peter Canon),* Stable Hand *(Elisha Cook).*

LOCATIONS: Nogales Mexico; Coronado National Forest; Old Tucson, Arizona.
A Solar-Fred Weintraub Production of a First Artists Presentation
SHOOTING TITLES: *I, Tom Horn; I, Tom Horn—A Last Will and Testament of the Old West; Horn.*

McQueen only wears one outfit through the whole movie, so you'd better like it.

Original ad art certainly lays it on the line. (All pictures copyright © 1980 by Warner Bros. Inc.)

MPAA rating: R.
Opened March 28, 1980 (98 minutes).

REVIEWS

"A sorry ending to the once high hopes of First Artists Productions. McQueen certainly looks like he's walking through the part and the picture as a whole is such a technical embarrassment the rest of the credits must have walked with him" *(Variety).*

"If McQueen doesn't appear to be acting, it's because—like Wayne and Cooper—he's learned to act this type of character so well, all theatrical trickery is virtually invisible. It's a genuinely fine piece of good filmmaking which does justice to any filmgoer's time. And it returns a genuine superstar to audiences after far too long an absence" (Robert Osborne, *Hollywood Reporter*).

In the long and soul-defeating interim between the making and the release of *An Enemy of the People*, a number of projects

McQueen, once having learned how to ride with one hand and shoot with the other for *Wanted: Dead or Alive* and *The Magnificent Seven*, slides easily back into the old routine. No doubling, natch.

appear, then fade. It is getting worse, and these two years will culminate in 1980 with McQueen's *Tom Horn*, a picture he doesn't even want to do, but must.

He has continued to look for properties that will star Ali and himself. *Nothing in Common* is suggested as a co-starrer by producer Tony Bill at Warners, but it founders. *Fancy Hardware* is tailored for them, but then it's retailored for Streisand and Travolta, who don't like it either. *The Missouri Breaks*, about a bounty hunter and an outlaw, is improbably written for them and director Bob Rafelson, but it goes instead to Brando, Nicholson, and director Arthur Penn. The Salkinds want him (and Redford, Hoffman, Streisand, Newman, Beatty, Raquel Welch, Michael York, Telly Savalas, and Shelley Winters) for their gigantic *Superman*, but none of the above gets into the picture, and the Salkinds turn McQueen down specifically because he's too fat. Once upon a time, producer Irwin Allen had offered McQueen $3 million to do the sequel to *The Towering Inferno*, but now his name isn't in the proposed credits, and the film never makes it past conception. Universal thinks about Steve and Ali for *Gable and Lombard*, but the word is Steve and Ali are in trouble (they are)

McQueen never allowed his slight stature to be pointed out on screen until *Tom Horn*. Here he actually underlines it as part of his characterization.

227

And just who was Tom Horn? A Pinkerton, a Rough Rider, a U.S. Cavalry scout to whom Geronimo surrendered. Your basic colorful figure of Ye Old West.

and so the parts go to James Brolin and Jill Clayburgh.

McQueen as Gable? Don't laugh. It's not the only time in his career he's heard this one. He leaves Marvin Josephson's Creative Management Associates before it merges with the International Famous Agency to become International Creative Management, but Josephson lures McQueen back into the agency fold by suggesting McQueen might have a good shot at playing Rhett Butler in Zanuck/Brown's *Tara: The Continuation of Gone With the Wind.*

In February, 1977, McQueen steps into *The Gauntlet,* which has been written for Streisand and Brando, but Brando has ankled the show, and it's open for McQueen. But Streisand doesn't want McQueen, she wants Clint Eastwood, who eventually takes over the whole project himself, and who co-stars Sondra Locke instead of Streisand. McQueen ends up having no participation in it at all.

McQueen continues his recent policy of being too expensive for anyone. Sir Lew Grade approaches him for *Raise the Titanic!,* but the pricetag is too high and the part goes to Richard Johnson, and the film sinks anyway. When things like that happen, McQueen knows that following his instinct is the right thing to do. He is briefly considered for what will become the Richard Dreyfuss part in *Close Encounters*

Hired by Wyoming land barons to wipe out cattle rustling, Horn succeeds too well, to the point where the land barons are afraid of him, turn on him, and frame him for a murder he hasn't committed. Here, handcuffed, he faces the prosecution alongside his defense lawyer (Harry Northup).

The former Linda Evenstad of Hartford, Connecticut, later a major television star on ABC's *Dynasty*. McQueen has this part custom-written for her, and Evans insists on deglamorizing the role, to the degree of wearing a gold tooth and no makeup.

of the Third Kind, but Columbia president Alan Hirschfield says that if the film itself does not attract an audience, then neither will McQueen's presence, and his fee is too high to boot. He is mentioned to play Ernest Hemingway in producer Jay Weston's film of Mary Welsh Hemingway's biography of her husband, but the project is indefinitely shelved.

Then, in August, 1979, he makes the richest actor's deal ever: $5 million to star in James Clavell's *Tai-Pan.* This time his name is on the dotted line, with Richard Fleischer directing, and over $18 million in foreign pre-sales are won using his name alone. Now $5 million is only the median figure given to the media. Initial guesses run in the $3 million range, and some estimates run as high as $10 million plus points, by far an industry record. One large payment of $1 million flat, non-returnable, has been made to McQueen, with a second chunk forthcoming on a contractually prearranged pay date, but when the second check is late, McQueen abruptly walks out of the production. He's a million dollars richer for having done absolutely nothing. This is a perfect job, he figures. Didn't want to take the trouble to do a movie anyhow. Just to rub it in, he announces publicly that his firm and implacable asking price for a film will be $5 million, and you'd better give him a nice percentage, too, and it

Of all McQueen's affairs, the one with Linda Evans was the briefest, but it was also the only one to get the girl a screen role, heretofore verboten for any McQueen female.

McQueen had to undergo severe physical retraining before he dares appear on screen before his fans again. He was unable to lose all 60 pounds he had gained over the past five years, and the effort showed on his face.

damn well better be out of the gross, not the net.

And he says he's going to start charging $50,000 just to read scripts.

Thus said, he becomes the highest paid actor in Hollywood history.

Ali, in the meantime, has developed Neile Adams Syndrome, which is to say she's fed up. Things have been bad since Steve moved out of the Trancas ranch and into the Beverly Wilshire during the traumatic shooting of *Enemy*. Steve's reclusive Garbo-itis is getting worse. He'll take a swing at anybody with a camera.

McGraw is still itching to act, which she hasn't done since *The Getaway* eight years before. This comes from living with a man who is obsessed with being the sole breadwinner. So when Sam Peckinpah calls her up and asks her to take the femme lead in his upcoming *Convoy*, an epic adaptation of the C.W. McCall trucker hit song, she jumps at the chance. Willingly she traipses the 800 miles to a difficult shoot in New Mexico. Her action is fully

and consciously against Steve's wishes—his orders, really. History repeats itself. Just as she walked out on Robert Evans for Steve McQueen, she is now doing it to McQueen. Hollywood karma.

McQueen goes for the grand slam. He travels to the Albuquerque location, quenching rumors of Ali's reputed affair on the set with some cast member. P. K. Strong, location coordinator for the picture, says it's an unfounded rumor, that McQueen got lonely and only wanted to see his wife. He brings her daisies, just as he always had them sent from Fashion Flowers on Rodeo Drive. Here, on a dusty Southwestern location, he gives her a handful in an empty beer can. It is here that they celebrate their fourth wedding anniversary.

It is also their last one. Soon after, tired of Ali's independent streak, he files for divorce and picks up the decree himself in Los Angeles Superior Court. He is so mad at her that he will not take calls from her. He changes her address so that she no longer gets mail delivered to a friend's gas station in Malibu, a tactic they had once adopted to guard the seclusion Ali now so desperately wants to escape.

Divorced for the second time, McQueen puts the breakup behind him, and decides it's time to get himself back into movies, to be seen again.

He proposes to First Artists that he do Harold Pinter's play *Old Times* with Faye Dunaway. The company does not think much of the idea and refuses to advance him the $250,000 he wants for development money. What else to do but sue? The case is settled when First Artists (gladly) and McQueen (reluctantly) agree to shoot *Tom Horn*. The Western is a project McQueen had expressed some mild interest in making some years before, but that was prior to his decision that he wants to do only classics. The *Horn* idea feels like a throwback, but at least it will fulfill his commitments to First Artists and to Warners. He wants to get out from under their hegemony so badly that he agrees. What guides him through it is that it will be the last First Artists production, and soon he will be free.

He becomes more involved when he manages to get his latest girlfriend, actress Linda Evans, into the film.

Oh, yes, he has wasted no post-Ali time. He

turned on the old McQ charm, and lured Evans away from her husband, Los Angeles realtor Stan Herman. She's a relatively obscure actress, who graduated from Hollywood High to become an MGM starlet. She has done only a few things, the ingénue Audra role on *The Big Valley*, a featured part as singer "Sugar Kane" in *Beach Blanket Bingo*, but she doesn't have much of a career. What there was was subverted in her first marriage to John Derek, whom she had landed as he was nursing his wounds suffered when wife number two, Ursula Andress, left him for Jean-Paul Belmondo. The tables were turned when he left Linda to take one 16-year-old Mary Cathleen Collins to Greece, where he transformed her into Bo Derek. Evans has just turned down the role of *The Bionic Woman*, and is up for grabs. Steve grabs her. He's counting on her getting him through the rigors of this latest picture.

As in any McQueen picture, the production inexplicably encounters nearly insurmountable difficulties. Originally scheduled to be shot way back in the summer of 1978, it has been postponed when TV enters the picture with rival productions. Universal has announced its TV-movie for NBC, *Tom Horn and the Apache Kid*, while ABC and producer Steve Forrest say they're bringing out their own version. Robert Redford's people declare he's to star in a United Artists film, with Sydney Pollack directing a William Goldman script. McQueen and Redford go eye to eye. Redford blinks first and drops out. Then CBS and Lorimar start work on a four-hour *Mr. Horn* with David Carradine playing the same William Goldman script written for Redford. First Artists gets a copy of *Mr. Horn* and decides that since it is about the Indian scout's younger years, and since McQueen's Horn is about the mature man facing the end of his life, that there is room in the world for two projects. The Warners edition commences shooting two weeks before the CBS version goes on the air to low ratings.

McQueen, though, is dissatisfied with the way the film is going and figures it's time to throw the legendary McQueen weight around. He doesn't like the Abe Polonsky script and orders constant rewrites, to the extent that the tone of the source novel by Will Henry is totally eradicated. Don Siegel (*Hell Is for Heroes*) is supposed to direct, but he's replaced by Elliott Silverstein, who leaves the film rapidly, sup-

planted by James William Guercio, who is fired and succeeded by TV director William Wiard, in charge of his first movie and directing a new script by Thomas McGuane.

Given these convolutions, it is no wonder that the film turns out to be terrible. Its theme, a myth about a man of genuine 19th-century rough-hewn honor trying to understand the changing rules of the 20th, is of value, but the treatment is inept.

Once in the editing room, two widely separate approaches are tried out. One tells the straight story all the way through, while the other takes the end of the film, breaks it up into pieces, and intersperses the pieces with flashbacks. The straightforward treatment wins out, but Warners is once again stumped as to how to sell it as a Steve McQueen film. They're facing an almost mandatory March,

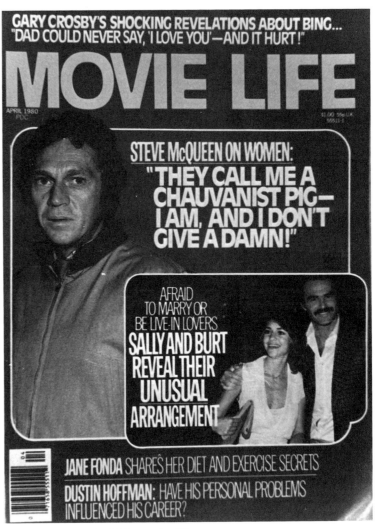

Weighty issues aside, McQueen is still a potent fan magazine draw (even if they did misspell his favorite word, chauvinist).

231

1980, release date, and three weeks before the opening, the wheels are still turning, trying to get the film into releasable shape. Producer Fred Weintraub, who has backed McQueen every step of the way, is frankly apprehensive, and prays the film will go on the strength of McQueen's name alone.

Warners sneaks the picture into Oxnard, 15 miles from McQueen's Santa Paula ranch. For the American public at large, it is the first view they have had of McQueen in over five years. His introductory shot is gorgeous: a slow zoom in on his profile under the titles, his face, the lines a little deeper since the last time we saw him, ruddily illuminated by the red sun in the east.

McQueen plays the part quietly, bluntly. If a fella's bothering a friend of his, why, he blows the fella's toes clean off. If a baddie shoots his beloved horse, what else can he do but shoot the baddie, giving him five slugs additional even after the villain's plainly dead, and then he burns a house down for good measure. In all he gets rid of seven transgressors, rather messily, and that's why the film gets an R rating, McQueen's first. McQueen acts it out so honorably, however, that he is by stretched definition a hero.

So McQueen himself is fine in it. He really is. He pulls the part off and makes you like him for doing it. But the picture is atrocious. The performances are flat, pedestrian, with lines delivered with no energy at all. The photography is dark and murky, and often the details of a face are obscured in shadow because the lighting is way off. The editing is awry, as in death scenes telegraphed by slow motion even before Horn shoots. No surprises. And it makes big mistakes, like giving Horn too-obvious lines like "I'm afraid to lose my ability to come and go as I please. I'm afraid of losing my freedom." Like a McQueen proverb, in italics.

Worst of all is a jailbreak sequence, when you think he's really going to turn into Steve McQueen and get out.

But he doesn't. They hang him. Can you believe it? They hang Steve McQueen! You keep expecting him to escape this scrape, and smile that McQueen grin when it's all over. You wait and you wait and you wait and nothing happens except that they get him in the end.

Stinks.

The Hunter

PARAMOUNT, 1980

His name is Papa Thorson.
He's funny. Gentle. Loveable.
And deadly.
So don't let
the bunny slippers
fool you.

STEVE McQUEEN is THE HUNTER

Production now completed.
Coming From Paramount
August, 1980.

Paramount Pictures Presents A Rastar-Mort Engelberg Production Starring Steve McQueen "The Hunter" Produced by Mort Engelberg Screenplay by Richard Levinson & William Link and Peter Hyams Directed by Buzz Kulik   Copyright © MCMLXXX by Paramount Pictures Corporation All Rights Reserved   A Paramount Picture

First ads conception stresses action and humor. (All pictures copyright © 1980 by Paramount Pictures Corporation)

CREDITS

Director, *Buzz Kulik;* producer, *Mort Engleberg;* screenplay, *Ted Leighton, Peter Hyams,* from the book by *Christopher Keane* and the life of *Ralph "Papa" Thorson;* photographer, *Fred Koenekamp* (Metrocolor, Panavision); editor, *Robert Wolfe;* production designer, *Ronald Hobbs;* music, *Michel Legrand;* costumes, *Tommy Welsh, Denita del Signore;* casting, *Jennifer Shull;* stunt coordinator, *Gary Combs;* technical advisor, *Ralph "Papa" Thorson.*

CAST

Ralph "Papa" Thorson *(STEVE McQUEEN),* Ritchie Blumenthal *(Eli Wallach),* Dotty *(Kathryn Harrold),* Tommy Price *(LeVar Burton),* Sheriff John Strong *(Ben Johnson),* Spota *(Richard Venture),* Rocco Mason *(Tracey Walter),* Bartender *(Ralph "Papa" Thorson),* Hustler *(Taurean Blacque),* Mike *(Christopher Keane).*

LOCATIONS: Kankakee and Chicago, Illinois.
A Rastar/Mort Engleberg Production.
SHOOTING TITLES: *The Bounty Hunter, Bounty, The Life of Ralph Thorson.*

MPAA rating: PG.
Opened July 28, 1980 (117 minutes).

REVIEWS

"A riveting new film, smashing action-adventure yarn colored with marvelously quirky humor" (Rona Barrett, "Good Morning America," ABC-TV)
"At 50, the actor's settled into a graceful middle-age. Although the lopsided smile and intense blue eyes remain unchanged, youthful cockiness has been replaced by a seasoned authority" (Stephen Schaefer, *Us*).

Tom Horn has, indeed, failed at the box office, but so anxious is McQueen to return to mainstream American cinema that he immediately goes back into another picture, back to back, something he has never done before, not even when he was a struggling young actor in the fifties.

The second approach pushes action alone.

Real hunter Ralph "Papa" Thorson plays a cameo in the movie. Never has suspension of disbelief been so blatant as audience's accepting McQueen, 5'6" and 150 pounds, as Thorson, 6'2" and 310 pounds. The author of Thorson's biography, Christopher Keane, also has a bit in the film, as "Mike."

He's not as fast as he used to be...
That's what makes him human.
He's a bounty hunter...
And that's what makes him dangerous.

STEVE McQUEEN AS **THE HUNTER**

The incredible true story of Ralph "Papa" Thorson, a modern-day bounty hunter.

Paramount Pictures Presents A Rastar/Mort Engelberg Production Steve McQueen as The Hunter Eli Wallach Kathryn Harrold LeVar Burton and Ben Johnson as Sheriff Strong Screenplay by Ted Leighton and Peter Hyams Music by Michel Legrand Produced by Mort Engelberg Directed by Buzz Kulik A Paramount Picture Copyright © MCMLXXX by Paramount Pictures Corporation, All Rights Reserved

PG PARENTAL GUIDANCE SUGGESTED
SOME MATERIAL MAY NOT BE SUITABLE FOR CHILDREN

Mort Engleberg, often paired with producer Ray Stark in rewarding projects, has brought McQueen a script about the famed modern-day bounty hunter Ralph "Papa" Thorson. Engleberg has been kicking around the idea for some time, once planning it as a Fox film to be directed by Michael Winner. McQueen likes the story so much he doesn't even charge Engleberg $50,000 to read it. He is captivated by the idea of playing his second biographical bounty-hunter part within a year. The script meets his approval, since it is written like an updated urban Western.

The possibilities are ripe: a contemporary hunter-for-hire, operating legally under a never-revoked 1872 law which asserts a bounty hunter may arrest, break and enter, cross state lines, do anything to bring back a criminal who has jumped bail, with no holds barred in the pursuit. Thorson, a great bear of a man, is responsible for bringing 5,000 fugitives back in from the cold, and he has become a kind of folk hero who has been the subject of an adulatory biography. The *Wanted: Dead or Alive* element appeals enormously to McQueen, and he believes he has at last found his come-back vehicle.

Free at last of Warners and the late First Artists, McQueen can now make a terrific independent deal for himself, and Paramount is more than willing to back him. His fee, unsurprisingly, is a knockout $3 million of the picture's $10.5 million budget. McQueen, for all that, goes into the thing so whole-heartedly,

Second picture for McQueen and Eli Wallach (first was *The Magnificent Seven*). Wallach plays his evasive boss.

Kathryn Harrold gets the girlfriend's part after Sally Field turned it down.

Ben Johnson, in his third appearance with McQueen, following *Junior Bonner* and *The Getaway*. As a Chicago sheriff he says, "Just look at us, an old sheriff and a bounty hunter, born a century too late." McQueen answers, "Nothing's changed. Just good guys and bad guys." And there you have the theme of the movie.

Papa's methods are quite direct. With LeVar Burton from *Roots*.

so professionally, that the movie will wrap four days early and $300,000 under budget.

Not to say the flick is not without its snags, but they are far from monumental. An initial script by Richard Levinson and William Link is forgotten. Paramount fires co-scripter and director Peter Hyams, and then seeks to instate McQueen as director. The issue comes up before the Directors Guild, and in a precedent-setting decision rules that "anyone assigned to or set to perform in a film cannot replace the director of that picture if they preceded the director in joining the production." McQueen is therefore ineligible to direct, but to everyone's surprise he takes the ruling in stride. He readily accepts the studio's next choice of director, Buzz Kulik, who has made a number of highly thought-of TV movies. So well does everyone get along that McQueen, Engleberg, and Kulik talk about doing a Western in Australia, *Quigley Down Under*. It will never be made.

The Hunter begins production September 10, 1979, in Chicago and Kankakee, with some pick-up shots later in Los Angeles. The filming goes without a hitch. Smooth all the way. For McQueen is sure that this is the film which will return him to the superstar spotlight.

Centerpiece to the film is the 14-minute chase, much like *Bullitt*. McQueen tails a murder suspect, and follows him over tenement rooftops, down to the street under the El tracks, and into a train. Outside, McQueen rides the roof of the train with the suspect below, shooting at him through the ceiling. When the train enters a tunnel, it gets hairier. The finale comes in a spiral parking building, as the kid steals a car while McQueen commandeers a tow truck. In a shot publicized not only by Paramount but also by the Illinois State Film Commission, the kid's car takes a multistory plunge into the Chicago River, straight

An expensive and irreplaceable collection of antique toys rented by the producers to show Papa's childlike side.

McQueen is soundly thrashed by a guy twice his size, but subdues him with a bean bag from a stun gun.

237

This black Trans-Am is McQueen's only means of pursuit in one sequence, and the gag that he can't drive is very funny.

down (like a similar stunt in *The Blues Brothers*).

Paramount has pencilled the film in as an August, 1980, release, but it is set to come out during a summer season when tried-and-true heavy-duty male stars are doing poor business: Clint Eastwood in *Bronco Billy*, John Travolta in *Urban Cowboy*, Burt Reynolds in *Rough Cut*. The he-men are not box-office this year. It is a strange quirk on the part of the American public, and to compensate Paramount pushes the release date up a couple of weeks into July.

Doesn't help. *The Hunter* is released and then withdrawn, disappearing without a trace, written off as a casualty of this maleless summer.

It is a heart-sickening blow to McQueen, who knows he has done good work. He was sure it was a perfect vehicle from both sides—something to please the following, something to satisfy his own needs as a performer.

The only thing that will make him happy is more money. Angrily he demands $5 million against 15 percent of the combined domestic and foreign grosses for his next movie. Even if his films are going to die, he will be well paid for them. These are the conditions he gives the producers of *Manhattan Project*, a nuclear terrorist melodrama to star Sophia Loren. Once again, the picture never sees fruition.

238

The strain of making two action films in a row shows in this 50-year-old man's face.

The thing he is most bitter about when he thinks about *The Hunter* is that he has finally become a character actor, which he has always wanted to be. His touch is everywhere, and he characterizes through detail. He drinks Budweiser, apple juice, Jack Daniels. He carries a .45, but always uses a stun gun to stress the non-killing side of his nature. He wears bunny slippers and collects antique toys; dogs don't like him, and he has to wear reading glasses. He's got a pregnant girlfriend in an on-again/off-again relationship. He's got a psycho speed freak gunning for him, and the guy is so far gone he makes Son of Sam seem sane. His cantankerous employer constantly welches on his debts, so he always has to take another job. When he's got nothing better to do, he rides the roofs of subway cars pursuing one mad killer or another.

Tremendous material, and McQueen plays it all tongue-in-cheek, not broadly but subtly, for the first time in his quarter-century career. Best of all, he insists on inserting a running in-joke making fun of the fact that poor Papa is such a rotten driver that he can't even park a car. McQueen drafts his own yellow '51 Chevy convertible for the film, and he looks right at home in it. A really good performance, completely wasted because nobody goes to see it. Yet it is the perfect mixture of what audiences expect and what he wants to do.

Too late. He has been absent from the screen too long, and his standing has been forgotten, his stardom usurped by new stars like Robert

The most talked-about sequence is a 14-minute chase through Chicago, recalling *Bullitt*. At one point, Papa hangs precariously from rushing subway car as a tunnel looms in the distance.

DeNiro, Roy Scheider, Al Pacino. He has wasted too much time on *An Enemy of the People*, stayed far too hermetic between movies. Audiences know his name; they just don't care anymore to see his movies.

It is a Hollywood horror story: he is a has-been. The highest-paid has-been in the business. Tinseltown has the last laugh, after all.

The movie ends on a wrenchingly ironic note. The ongoing theme of his girlfriend's pregnancy puts him in an emergency room in the final moments of the movie, waiting for her to deliver after an agonizing trip by car to the hospital. The nurse comes out to tell him

mother and baby are doing fine, but spots him lying out cold on the tile floor of the receiving area. It is a comic touch, a light way to end the movie, but it is still an arresting shock to see McQueen lying like that on the floor, his eyes closed. He doesn't even get the last line.

Producers Herb Jaffe and Jerry Beck have inquired of McQueen's representatives whether he would be interested in doing their *Hang Tough* yarn by Elmore Leonard, about a tenacious Detroit detective hot after redneck killers.

The agents say no. They know something no one else does yet. Steve McQueen has made his last movie. He is dying.

The End

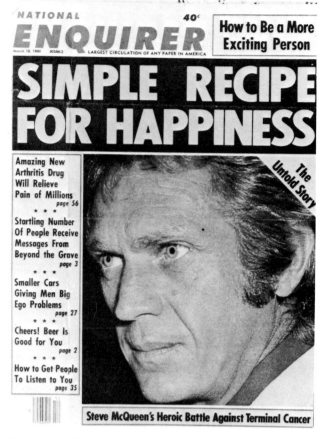

The *National Enquirer* breaks the story on March 18, 1980. McQueen vigorously denies it.

Would that *The Steve McQueen Story* could end with the hero going out the way he came in, full of glory and vinegar. A formula race car crash would have done the job nicely, or a spectacular bike spill.

Instead Steve McQueen's life ends because of a very rare lung ailment called mesothelioma, and the way he deals with his illness focuses the world's attention on him the way he has hoped his comeback vehicles would. He goes out, all right, but it is in a bizarre panoply of flashbulbs and pathos.

The end begins in December, 1979, as McQueen has just finished shooting *The Hunter*. He's talking with old *Wanted: Dead or Alive* stuntman buddy Charles Bail, now a writer-director, about doing *The Last Ride*, to focus on a cross-country bike race set in the fifties. Friends and crew have noticed how tired the actor looks, and in particular his girlfriend Barbara Minty is encouraging him to seek some kind of medical treatment. McQueen has split with Linda Evans, following the failure of *Tom Horn*, and has taken up again with Minty, a young model whom he had been seeing in Los Angeles after Ali and before Linda. Now it is Minty who manages to coax him into seeing a doctor, and wearily he acquiesces.

It is not well known, but McQueen has had a genuine terror of doctors and surgery. He has previously gone to the ends of the earth just to avoid the dentist. He is familiar with hiding illness. Bike racing had already severely impaired his hearing in the early seventies, and he refused then to have any kind of surgery, never, never, never, he said, to "go under the knife." He lost Yucatan because he wouldn't have an operation to correct his deafness.

Nevertheless convinced that he is suffering only from the exhaustion of making two demanding pictures in a row, he checks into Los Angeles' Cedars-Sinai Medical Center.

A few tests, and they know he has cancer.

It is a cancer that has been exacerbated by his two-pack-a-day smoking habit, which he has tried to kick many times, but it has actually been caused by his racing. The asbestos padding he used for years to insulate himself inside his formula racers is the culprit. An authority on mesothelioma, or cancer of the lung lining which McQueen has inarguably

240

Steve McQueen's Heroic Battle Against Terminal Cancer

Frantic last-ditch efforts by doctors have failed to halt a vicious and inoperable lung cancer that is killing Steve McQueen.

The end could come within two months, believes one of his doctors. But the steely-eyed screen hero is battling back bravely.

Soon after specialists broke the terrible news to McQueen in late December, he married his live-in love, Barbara Minty. Refusing to give an inch to his terminal illness, Steve is up at the crack of dawn — working on his ranch and flying antique airplanes.

But insiders have noticed one remarkable change in the 49-year-old actor.

Gone is the fiery Hollywood rebel and in his place is a subdued, deeply religious man who has clearly "made his peace with God."

The intense drama began December 18 when McQueen — who had been a heavy smoker until he quit about a year ago — collapsed gasping for breath and was rushed to Cedars-Sinai Medical Center in Los Angeles.

While the world was told he was suffering from bronchial pneumonia, McQueen secretly underwent extensive tests and exploratory surgery.

By TONY BRENNA & DONNA ROSENTHAL

January: "There is nothing we can do for him."

In late February, after the cobalt treatment failed to shrink the cancer, the surgeon added:

"There is absolutely no hope. It's a matter of two months at most."

But from the very first day in December when doctors told him there was little they could do, McQueen has acted like anything but a condemned man.

On January 16, he married girlfriend Barbara Minty at port where he has his own hangar. While Steve did loops and turns in the bright California sky. It's clear they plan to make every moment together can join her husband in the nally ill man — gets up at the crack of dawn and works around the ranch before he

STILL FLYING HIGH, McQueen defies his illness by throwing himself into flying antique planes. New bride Barbara Minty watches as he prepares to take off.

The *Enquirer* article, with photo of McQueen and two-month bride Minty, posed inside one of his new biplanes, his latest speed craze.

contracted, links the disease overwhelmingly to the inhalation of the microscopic asbestos fibers which McQueen has been breathing in for the last 25 years. There is no doubt of the nature of the disease or what has caused it. The disease and its generator have been known since 1898, as is the discomforting fact that his cigarette smoking has increased his risk of contraction by 55 times. Who knows how much more harm his dope-smoking has caused? He'd been toking Luckies and pot for 25 years. But mesothelioma, a very slow-growth disease, has taken this long to show up. There has never been a hint of it before. But now it has hit him, and hit hard.

There is no cure. He has no choice but to submit to surgery. Radioactive cobalt is implanted in his chest cavity, and a month later, when he returns to Cedars-Sinai for more exploratory surgery, the doctors find that the cobalt has failed to stop the now rampant spread of the cancer.

A month later, on January 16, 1980, on his Santa Paula ranch 50 miles northwest of Los Angeles, he takes Barbara Minty, 25, as his third wife. Given the severity of his infirmity, life with Barbara is the only thing that makes

The follow-up comes six months later, and this time there is no choice but to admit that McQueen is a terminal case.

People pushes Liz and her latest beau. But at least McQueen's name is still above the title.

him happy. Three days after the wedding, Neile marries businessman Alvin Toffel, and the happy couples exchange friendly and heartfelt congratulations.

Then the *National Enquirer* gets wind of Steve's being sick, and breaks the story to a shocked country in a March, 1980, story, coinciding with the release of *Tom Horn*. McQueen's press coterie denies the story emphatically, admitting the actor has been hospitalized but only for viral pneumonia. The public buys it, especially when they read McQueen is considering suing the paper, a favorite Hollywood celebrity pasttime. When his friends hear that, they believe the lies he tells them.

Actually he is trying to figure out how to hold on to life. He has given up hope of finding salvation in the orthodox medical community, and begins looking outside it. He has studied the literature, and thinks he knows what he wants to do. For the first time in his life, he gives up his heavy indulgent drinking.

Then he hears about Dr. William Donald Kelley's nontoxic cancer therapy.

The circus has begun.

Kelley is a Texas dentist whose license was once suspended for five years by the Texas State Dentist Examining Board. Cited by a

Desperate cancer patients are flocking to Mexican hospitals seeking McQueen's therapy

Steve McQueen: Virtual prisoner in his hospital bungalow.

HUNDREDS of desperate cancer victims from around the world are rushing to northern Mexico and paying up to $500 a day in the hope of finding a last-minute cure, following the news of Steve McQueen's unconventional treatment for a rare form of the disease.

Near-terminal patients from all over America, as well as from Europe, Scandinavia, the Middle East and South America, have

near the center of the hospital complex.

He rarely ventures outside and if he wants to get some sun, he insists that a shield be set up outside the front door to guard him from prying eyes.

Recently, he has been leaving the clinic at weekends for short trips up and down the coast.

When McQueen arrived at Plaza Santa Maria in late July, he was virtually a stretcher case. American doctors had given him only weeks to live and he checked

free from all pain and will soon be able to see friends and visitors.

At the Plaza Santa Maria, McQueen wakes at 7 a.m. and has

Media coverage like this swamps Mexican clinics and gives the ill new hope.

Texas court in 1970 for practicing medicine without a license, he is also prohibited from distributing his book *One Answer to Cancer* in the state. The American Cancer Society has branded Kelley's work worthless.

McQueen meets Dr. Kelley for the first time in April, 1980, in Washington state. This first encounter with Kelley is made clandestinely under the name Don Schoonover, and the doctor is astonished to learn who his patient really is.

The purpose of the meeting is to introduce Steve to a system Kelley has developed at his International Health Institute in Dallas. "My technique," Kelley informs McQueen, "is based upon the assumption that if a person gives his or her body the nutrients it needs, and relieves its structural problems, stimulates the glands to do their jobs, cleanses out any accumulated toxins and maintains the proper mental and emotional states, the body will be able to handle all sorts of problems." Despite Kelley's legal problems with Texas medical authorities, McQueen has to admit that the approach sounds very right to him. The two men talk for hours into the night on the doctor's 160-acre farm in Winthrop, and they formulate a plan to shuttle McQueen incognito into the Plaza Santa Maria sanatorium near Rosarita, Mexico.

Some of his former patients write to Steve and Barbara, who are amazed at the unusual high spirits with which those stricken have responded to the Kelley System. Barbara is convinced Steve has wasted months of his life drinking and bewailing his condition, and that the rejuvenation effects alone may help Steve regain his strength.

Sobered, McQueen makes the journey to Mexico. The clinic, until just a few months previous a quiet resort, is 35 miles south of Tijuana, on the road to Ensenada. By the time McQueen arrives on July 31, he has developed secondary tumors in his stomach, and the disease has spread throughout the pleural membranes. He is admitted on a stretcher, Barbara by his side. He is put under the care of the clinic's director, Dr. Rodrigo Rodriguez, who places his patient on 30 grains of codeine a day to combat the pain. When the pain subsides, the treatment begins.

If McQueen wanted unorthodox, he gets it in Mexico. He wakes at seven, goes to bed at midnight. In between he is given 50 to 100 pills a day—vitamins, minerals, supplements. He is forbidden any red meat or animal-derivative foods, yet he is also given German sheep embryo injections. Laetrile is applied. So is Gerovital, claimed to retard the aging process, and a Japanese vaccine made from bacilli usually used in the treatment of tuberculosis. There is a weekly "junk-out" day when patients can reasonably stuff themselves on anything they want, but Steve is still much too weak to join them. Barbara stays with him. He undergoes more: coffee and lemon juice enemas, saunas, extensive chiropractic sessions, and on and on and on.

Miraculously, incredibly, he begins to improve, to the extent of making short trips up and down the Baja coast. Much of his renewed sense of well-being has come from the drastic detoxification program at the clinic, which has rid his body of impurities that block treatment.

When he returns from one of his jaunts, he discovers that the media are camped out on his front porch with all their paraphernalia: cameras, boom microphones, tape recorders, and he learns third-hand that his story is being featured in tabloids everywhere. His cover is broken, and in the midst of his healing he is surrounded by the pseudo-fans he has been seeking for the past five years. It has taken cancer to get them interested again.

All he wants, all he has ever wanted his whole life, is to be left alone. He sees, though, that there is no way out, and so on October 2, he allows his long-time publicist Warren Cowan to release the story: Steve McQueen is fighting cancer and intends to beat it. McQueen's official statement reads, in part, "The reason I denied that I had cancer was to save my family and friends from personal hurt and to retain my sense of dignity." That is gone now.

In an attempt to get the press off his back, he approaches a reporter from Televisa, the Mexican broadcast network, and makes an audio tape. In it he thanks his doctors, saying, "Congratulations to your country on your magnificent work." He goes on to say that the treatment "has given me an extraordinarily improved quality of life," that "I believe I will recover." He also begs people to stay away and leave him alone, hoping that "the cheap scandal sheets and curiosity seekers will not try to seek me out so I can continue my treatment."

While McQueen did get religious near the end, there was no end to sensationalizing the private death.

Alternative medical magazines such as this one probed his strange demise, seeking to take a stand one way or another, for or against his unusual therapy.

At the end, he says, "To all my fans and all my friends, keep your fingers crossed and keep the good thoughts coming. All my love and God bless you all. This is Steve McQueen." He sounds like a frail 70-year-old man doing a bad Steve McQueen vocal imitation.

The few seconds of this tape are broadcast worldwide. They are this weak, sad little man's final words to his public.

The carnival goes on. The tape only spurs the morbid. Sick and tired, literally and figuratively, Steve abandons the Plaza Santa Maria and heads back to his California ranch. There, intending to spend his last days having a good time, he gorges himself, really pigs out all the way, and once again it is Barbara who saves him from killing himself on junk food. She makes him try one last time, and because he is living on will and will alone—"I'm going out kicking and screaming every inch of the way!"—he takes the pseudonym Sam Sheppard

and checks into the Eastwood Hospital Clinic in El Paso for a CAT (Computerized Axial Topography) Scan. On the following Tuesday, November 4, he checks into the Santa Rosa Clinic in Juarez, right across the border, and has a small tumor removed from his neck.

He has three more days to live.

He weighs, they say, only a hundred pounds. His stomach is grotesquely bloated and he looks pregnant. His legs are so spindly they will not support him. He is still all there mentally, every cell battling to stay alive. He is astonished to learn that his nontoxic cancer therapy

244

has inspired thousands of patients to flee south of the border in last-ditch attempts to conquer their cancers, just as he is doing. The flood is awesome, and soon every sanatorium is packed with desperate, bright-eyed Americans seeking the same kind of cure they think McQueen has undergone. He thinks he may have done some good with his life, after all. He has been seeking comfort from Middletown, New Jersey, evangelist Lydia Stalnaker, but he derives greater comfort from this information. Suddenly he is calm.

On November 7, he must undergo radical surgery to excise an abdominal tumor. His surgeon, heart and kidney specialist Dr. Cesar Santos Vargas removes it. It weighs a crippling five pounds, and Dr. Fernando Hernandez says it is the worst case of cancer he has ever seen.

There is now more cancerous tissue than healthy tissue in McQueen's failing body. On top of that, he has a heart attack right there in the operating room.

McQueen, his will stronger than tempered steel, lasts another 16 hours. It seems impossible. Finally, his body's need to die overcomes his spirit's burn to survive, and he suffers a second heart attack. It is over.

Barbara is there, with his children, Terri, 21, and Chad, 19. They are at his bedside when he dies. Neile is absent; she has denounced the clinic and its doctors as "charlatans and exploiters."

The body is taken to the Prado Funeral Home in Juarez, where the necessary papers to transport it across the border are signed. An unmarked station wagon carries the remains from Juarez to a private airport in El Paso, where a Lear Jet is chartered to fly the plain brass-handled casket back to Los Angeles.

The funeral takes place four days later on the Santa Paula ranch. Barbara, Terri, and Chad are present the whole time, Neile and Ali have both been by earlier in the day. During the simple service, a group of eight antique biplanes flies over in a cross formation. The center plane is McQueen's last internal combustion toy, a chrome yellow PT-17 Stearman flown in memoriam by his friend Larry Endicott, who dips his wings as he passes over the funeral site.

There are no funereal flowers at the ranch. According to his wishes, if people want to remember him they should do so by sending

Even after his death, Steve McQueen still makes headlines.

donations to Boys Republic at Chino, Gary Avenue and Peyton Road, Chino CA 91710. He himself has left them $200,000.

In town, the Hollywood Wax Museum is forced to retire its Steve McQueen mannequin, because the influx of cards and flowers has filled the set and obscured the sightlines. Concern for the safety of the wax figure at the hands of crazed souvenir hunters also prompts its removal. Nostalgia shops report a heretofore unprecedented run on their files, as grieving fans buy up any picture they can find of their idol, especially bike shots from *The Great Escape* and car photos from *Bullitt*.

The funeral is only a service. There is no burial. There will be no tombstone. Nothing.

As he has asked—demanded probably, knowing him—his body has been cremated, and the planes that have just flown over are headed out to the Pacific Ocean. They will scatter his ashes, over the water, about forty miles directly west of Hollywood, as the sun is setting.

United Artists
joins the industry
in expressing regrets
on the passing of
Steve McQueen

United Artists
A Transamerica Company

UA is the only studio to publish a public display of grief.

Even after his death, Steve McQueen still makes headlines. Ali MacGraw cried out harshly on "Entertainment Tonight" against the flood of media coverage: "The most important thing in his life was his personal dignified privacy. He was too weak to combat the kind of invasion he was experiencing. It made all of us who loved him crazy. I still have an amazing amount of anger at a magazine that ran a picture of him after he died. I don't understand it. The hurt is so monumental, to be raped that way."

Steve McQueen
on Steve McQueen

"Sometimes I wish I was Jack Warner's son and didn't have to work."

"I want to get some sugar out of this business and run like a thief. I don't want to die with a martini in my hand."

"An actor is a puppet, manipu-
lated by a dozen other people.
Auto racing has dignity. But you
need the same absolute concentration. You have to reach insider
yourself and bring forth a lot of
broken glass."

"*I have to be careful be-cause I'm a limited ac-tor. I mean my range isn't very great. There's a whole lot of stuff I can't do, so I have to find characters and sit-uations that feel right. Even then, when I've got something that fits, it's a hell of a lot of work. I'm not a serious actor. There's something about my shaggy-dog eyes that makes people think I'm good. I'm not all that good.*"

"I like to eat at six,
go for a ride on my motorcycle,
and go to sleep."

"I don't believe in that phony hero stuff."

"If I hadn't made it as an actor, I might have wound up a hood."

"I believe in me.
God'll be No. 1 as long as I'm No. 1.
I'm a little screwed-up
but I'm beautiful."

FREE!

Citadel Film Series Catalog

From James Stewart to Moe Howard and The Three Stooges, Woody Allen to John Wayne, The Citadel Film Series is America's largest film book library.

Now with more than 125 titles in print, books in the series make perfect gifts—for a loved one, a friend, or yourself!

We'd like to send you, free of charge, our latest full-color catalog describing the Citadel Film Series in depth. To receive the catalog, call 1-800-447-BOOK or send your name and address to:

Citadel Film Series/Carol Publishing Group
Distribution Center B
120 Enterprise Avenue
Secaucus, New Jersey 07094

The titles you'll find in the catalog include:
The Films Of...

Alan Ladd
Alfred Hitchcock
All Talking! All Singing!
 All Dancing!
Anthony Quinn
The Bad Guys
Barbara Stanwyck
Barbra Streisand:
 The First Decade
Barbra Streisand:
 The Second Decade
Bela Lugosi
Bette Davis
Bing Crosby
Black Hollywood
Boris Karloff
Bowery Boys
Brigitte Bardot
Burt Reynolds
Carole Lombard
Cary Grant
Cecil B. DeMille
Character People
Charles Bronson
Charlie Chaplin
Charlton Heston
Chevalier
Clark Gable
Classics of the Gangster
 Film
Classics of the Horror Film
Classics of the Silent Screen
Cliffhanger
Clint Eastwood
Curly: Biography of a
 Superstooge
Detective in Film
Dick Tracy
Dustin Hoffman
Early Classics of the
 Foreign Film

Elizabeth Taylor
Elvis Presley
Errol Flynn
Federico Fellini
The Fifties
The Forties
Forgotten Films
 to Remember
Frank Sinatra
Fredric March
Gary Cooper
Gene Kelly
Gina Lollobrigida
Ginger Rogers
Gloria Swanson
Great Adventure Films
Great British Films
Great French Films
Great German Films
Great Romantic Films
Great Science Fiction Films
Great Spy Films
Gregory Peck
Greta Garbo
Harry Warren and the
 Hollywood Musical
Hedy Lamarr
Hello! My Real Name Is
Henry Fonda
Hollywood Cheesecake:
 60 Years of Leg Art
Hollywood's Hollywood
Howard Hughes in Hollywood
Humphrey Bogart
Ingrid Bergman
Jack Lemmon
Jack Nicholson
James Cagney
James Stewart
Jane Fonda
Jayne Mansfield

Jeanette MacDonald and
 Nelson Eddy
Jewish Image in American
 Films
Joan Crawford
John Garfield
John Huston
John Wayne
John Wayne Reference
 Book
John Wayne Scrapbook
Judy Garland
Katharine Hepburn
Kirk Douglas
Lana Turner
Laurel and Hardy
Lauren Bacall
Laurence Olivier
Lost Films of the
 Fifties
Love in the Film
Mae West
Marilyn Monroe
Marlon Brando
Moe Howard and The
 Three Stooges
Montgomery Clift
More Character People
More Classics of the
 Horror Film
More Films of the '30s
Myrna Loy
Non-Western Films of
 John Ford
Norma Shearer
Olivia de Havilland
Paul Newman
Paul Robeson
Peter Lorre
Pictorial History of Science
 Fiction Films

Pictorial History of Sex
 in Films
Pictorial History of War
 Films
Pictorial History of the
 Western Film
Rebels: The Rebel Hero
 in Films
Rita Hayworth
Robert Redford
Robert Taylor
Ronald Reagan
The Seventies
Sex in the Movies
Sci-Fi 2
Sherlock Holmes
Shirley MacLaine
Shirley Temple
The Sixties
Sophia Loren
Spencer Tracy
Steve McQueen
Susan Hayward
Tarzan of the Movies
They Had Faces Then
The Thirties
Those Glorious Glamour Years
Three Stooges Book of Scripts
Three Stooges Book of Scripts,
 Vol. 2
The Twenties
20th Century Fox
Warren Beatty
W. C. Fields
Western Films of John Ford
West That Never Was
William Holden
William Powell
Woody Allen
World War II